ABOUT T[...]

John McShane is a journalist and author. As a Fleet Street reporter and then associate editor in charge of news at both the *Daily Mirror* and the *Sunday Mirror* he has investigated many of the major crime stories of recent years. He is married with three children and has homes in London and Spain.

913 000 00099633

KNIFE CRIME

John McShane

Quercus

First published 2010 by

Quercus
21 Bloomsbury Square
London
WC1A 2NS

Copyright © 2010 by John McShane

Pictures on plate section page 6 top, 7 top
and page 8 © Ferrari Press Agency

A CIP catalogue record for this book is available
from the British Library

ISBN 978 1 84724 979 1

10 9 8 7 6 5 4 3 2 1

Typeset by Ellipsis Books Limited, Glasgow

Printed and bound in Great Britain by Clays Ltd, St Ives plc

To all who have suffered loss

PROLOGUE

Knives kill. They take life in the dead of an inner-city night or the broad daylight of a crowded shopping centre, in the alcohol-soaked anger of a packed bar or the innocence of a train filled with holidaymakers. Even outside a school, a place of learning for children. It makes no difference. The thrust of sharpened steel into a human being has the same terrible impact no matter where or when it happens. The victim could be known to the attacker or a complete stranger – assaulted by a person who had entered their life mere moments earlier, with fatal, horrific results. That makes no difference either. The blood-soaked consequences are the same, the grief of the victim's loved ones is universal.

The cases that are examined in this book show how suddenly the smallest dispute can escalate into death, how random fate can be when it comes to choosing the next victim. They also show the havoc that a knife in the wrong hands can cause to the human body.

The use of knives, so easy to obtain from any kitchen drawer, is a growing problem, not confined just to teenage gangs but for anyone who walks the streets of Britain. Everyone is a potential victim. Those unknown footsteps heard approaching from behind might be innocent, or they might be something more deadly . . .

The increasing menace isn't just an urban myth, either. Those who might dismiss public fear as paranoia whipped up by an excitable media, need only to listen to pronouncements from on high and look at the official statistics to feel a sense of foreboding.

Even Prime Minister Gordon Brown, announcing an extra £5 million to be spent on tackling knife crime and serious youth violence in the spring of 2009, had to admit: 'Knife crime and all forms of serious youth violence damage communities, destroy lives, and rob families of hope. It is completely unacceptable.'

As if to illustrate the havoc that can result from the wrong knife in the wrong hands, a major report on the crisis soon afterwards revealed that children as young as seven were being used like 'golf caddies' to transport knives for older youths. The belief that knives were more widespread than ever motivated an 'arms' race' by young gang members, a Home Affairs Committee of MPs said, and subsequently very young children were transporting the blades in order that their elders could try to escape being caught.

The figures bring a chill to the blood. The MPs who

had been investigating the growing menace said there had been 270 stabbing deaths in 2008 and many young people thought it now normal to be armed with a blade in modern Britain. The committee report called for more knife-carriers to be locked up, and pointed out that the number of knife deaths had risen by 27 per cent in the preceding two years and was at its highest since records began in 1977. Other figures were equally alarming: serious stabbing injuries needing hospital treatment soared nearly 50 per cent in the previous ten years to 5,239 in 2008, one in three eleven- to sixteen-year-olds had carried a knife in the previous year, rising to six in ten among kids suspended from school. Up to 85 per cent of children who carried knives said they did so for protection.

The MPs said most knife-carriers who were caught should be given prison sentences, yet only one in five of those caught with a knife was being jailed, and more knife-carriers were given cautions than imprisoned. The report said in the last three months of 2008, of the 6,704 people caught with knives only 1,386 were given an immediate custodial sentence. Forcing someone else to carry a blade earned a maximum four years in prison having been made a crime in 2007, but no one was prosecuted that year and the figures for 2008 were not known. The MPs backed police using stop-and-search, saying the fear of getting caught was a deterrent, and they also pointed out knife crime was costing the UK a staggering £1.25 billion a year. So frightening was the situation that the MPs even called for lessons in school for all eleven-year-olds on the horrors of knife crime. Let that sink in for a moment; small children in a class-room who should be being taught about all that is good in life have, instead, to be warned off that which is evil.

Committee chairman Keith Vaz painted a depressing picture of a nation on the brink when he pointed out youngsters did not feel protected by parents or the police, saying: 'Young people carry knives because they fear that others are carrying knives. This spiralling of knife possession puts all young people at risk. Too many tragic deaths have occurred because of this. We have to stop this arms race. Some young people feel the need to protect themselves with knives. We are clearly fail-ing them. Children, of all people, should not feel unsafe in our society.'

The MPs also stated the obvious: that a great deal of the knife violence in modern Britain was down to the growing gang culture in the country, although cutting down the supply of knives alone would not solve the problem, as most often it was a kitchen knife that was used. More prison programmes to tackle offending behaviour were needed plus 'interventions' with young people in danger of more serious offending.

Shadow Home Secretary Chris Grayling said: 'The committee is absolutely right to say that we need to tackle the root social causes of knife crime. But we've also got to be much tougher on those committing acts of antisocial behaviour to prevent them from going on to commit more serious offences, like knife crime, later in life.'

Less than two weeks after that summer report there was more disturbing news when fresh figures from the Ministry of Justice confirmed that only a fifth of criminals caught with a knife or offensive weapon in England and Wales were sent to prison immediately, and a quarter of knife offenders were let off with a caution. In the first three months of 2009, criminals committed 6,477 offences involving knives or other weapons – that works out at over seventy a day. Of that immense figure, 1,320 were given immediate custody by the courts, with a larger number, 1,599, cautioned. A third of offenders were handed community sentences.

These figures were just the latest in a seemingly endless list of statistics on the knife crime problem; some claimed the battle against knives was being won, others indicated it was a losing fight.

If ever there were proof that the Victorian prime minister Benjamin Disraeli was right when he said 'There are three kinds of lies: lies, damned lies, and statistics', then the figures on knife crime prove the accuracy of his words.

The most memorable example was in December 2008 when the then Home Secretary Jacqui Smith released figures depicting a positive situation in the war against knives, only famously and humiliatingly to have to quickly backtrack in the Commons, saying the Home Office had been 'too quick off the mark'. Her climb-down came after Sir Michael Scholar, head of the independent UK Statistics Authority, had said the claims were 'premature, irregular and selective'.

In the midst of the avalanche of reports – many of them conflicting – million-pound-plus initiatives, mind-boggling figures, various campaigns by the Home Office, the police and newspapers in addition to numerous knife amnesties, the nightmare continued. Every day seemed to bring a new horror story, and possibly even more disturbing was the knowledge that many attacks with knives attracted little or no publicity, assuming they had even been reported in the first place. In some cases the torment of the victim's loved ones understandably attracted widespread attention and sympathy. Many others, however, would go unrecorded or barely noticed.

But one thing was certain beyond all doubt. Those who suffered either directly or through the irreplaceable loss of one dear to them, would never, could never, forget the day that knife crime came into their lives.

1

Ben Kinsella's savage knife murder was not unique. Far from it. In fact, it mirrored a bloodstained catalogue of numerous violent deaths in Britain in recent years. The similarities between Ben's killing and many, too many, others are undeniable: a knife assault with the blade thrust deeply into the victim's body. A late-night inner-city clash in which a totally innocent young man was to lose his life. Cowardly young attackers, motivated by 'reasoning' that no sane, civilised person could comprehend. Teenage thugs who already had records of violence, as if in some sick rehearsal for their ultimate deed. No sign of regret on the part of the killers over the consequences of their violence. Condemnation from all quarters of the 'animals' who carried out the crime and bewilderment at their barbarity.

And of all the themes that run through the deaths, there was the most heartbreaking common factor of them all: the grief of the victim's family.

The uncomprehending bewilderment, the tears, the loss and the anger over a loved one who had left home one day never to return. Taken from them by forces beyond their control and which any intelligent human being would struggle to understand. No matter how often so many of the aspects of that scenario have been repeated, the emptiness felt by those left behind remains theirs and theirs alone. Although a universal feeling of loss pervades every case, the sorrow felt by each family is unique to them. No one else knows exactly the pain they feel. There may be similarities, true, but the exact nature of their suffering can never be duplicated.

Ben Kinsella, an Arsenal fan who had once been in an episode of *The Bill*, was just sixteen when he died, a bright young boy who had gone out locally with friends to celebrate completing his GCSEs. He had passed ten of them, with A*s in art and media and As in English language and literature. He was not to live long enough even to find out his results – his life was to end that night.

One of the ironies of his death is that just a few weeks before that deadly night, he had written to Prime Minister Gordon Brown asking him to tackle the problem of knife crime. It was part of a school project, and in it he accused the government of standing by as young people were dying, warning, with a prophetic grimness, that violence was becoming 'part of our culture'.

Ben wrote: 'Problems like this will continue to grow unless change starts to happen. Society needs to see a difference before it's too late. Youth violence hits deadly peak. When will it stop?'

He even penned an essay, chillingly written just six weeks before his death as part of a school project, describing in detail what it would be liked to be stabbed and how he would feel looking at his killer as the blood ebbed from his body.

Ben could not have known he was uncannily predicting the night of 29 June 2008, in Islington – a fashionable area of north London where politicians and media folk lived in stylish multimillion-pound homes alongside an underclass on nearby council estates. He had no idea that into his life that evening would come three savage young men who were to show brutality to him that, even in an age that had tragically become accustomed to casual, needless violence, still shocked.

The beginning of the end of Ben's life came after swaggering bully Jade Braithwaite started rowing with one of Ben's friends because he felt he had been 'disrespected' by a look he had been given at Shillibeers bar, a popular nightspot with young people in the area.

The six foot seven inches tall Braithwaite said: 'I've got my tool [weapon] on me, and it will open you up. I'll stab people up.' Then he telephoned his friends

Juress Kika and Michael Alleyne asking them to 'back him' in his planned vengeful attack.

When the deadly, hooded trio had linked up they saw Ben – who had not been involved in the disturbance – and his friends walking home and gave chase. Ben was told by a friend 'Run, run, they have a knife', and Ben said to the young monsters, 'What are you coming over to me for? I haven't done anything wrong.' That made no difference to Braithwaite who kicked him in the stomach, knocking him over. They surrounded Ben and stabbed him, leaving blood everywhere. CCTV footage later released to the world saw Ben staggering out from the parked van and car he had been trapped between, blood from the eleven wounds he had suffered in just a few seconds covering his yellow shirt. His heart was punctured and a rib behind it was split. Two more knife blows plunged into his lungs.

He told his friends he had been stabbed and one of them, Louis, the son of *Birds of a Feather* actress Linda Robson, cradled him and slapped him in an attempt to keep him conscious. His pals called an ambulance in a desperate attempt to save his life, but five hours later Ben was dead.

He was the seventeenth youngster to be murdered in London that year, and even though it was only midsummer he was the twelfth to be fatally knifed. That alone would have ensured his death would attract attention, but the fact that his sister, Brooke Kinsella, was a young actress who had played Kelly Taylor in the BBC's popular soap opera *EastEnders*, ensured the murder dominated the headlines.

Brooke, twenty-four, summoned up the courage to say the next day, 'Yesterday, we tragically lost not only a beautiful son and brother, but a true angel. He was one of the kindest and gentlest boys God created.' Calling for an end to such crimes she said, 'Now it truly is the time to stand up and put an end to this. We always knew that Ben would make a special mark in this world. Although it is in the worst possible circumstances, hopefully he will be the one to put an end to this. My family are determined to fight in his memory to make the streets safe for our children. Please, boys and girls, put down your knives and weapons and think about the pain and suffering they will cause.'

The actress also urged parents to talk to their children over the issue of knife crime: 'Please can we waste no more time and come together as a country to ensure that no other lives are wasted.'

Even as she was speaking it was revealed that more than 1,000 people had been arrested in London in a six-week anti-knife operation after police carried out 26,777 stop-and-searches and recovered 528 weapons as part of Operation Blunt Two. Mayor Boris Johnson announced the progress of the Operation with Met. Commissioner Sir Ian Blair, and urged parents, siblings and friends to 'shop' those youths who they know regularly carry knives. He said: 'We cannot win this battle alone, we're going to need your support.'

The men who stabbed Ben Kinsella wouldn't be among those taking heed of those words, however. They inhabited a different world, away from civilised society. Jade Braithwaite, who instigated the attack, was known on the street as J-Man. He was a drug-dealer who had been locked up for a year after robbing a teenager of a laptop. His sentence was cut to a community order even though he had been labelled 'cowardly and vicious' by his trial judge.

Juress Kika had the street name Dubzy. At the age of eleven he started to amass a string of convictions and cautions involving assault, drugs, robbery, resisting arrest and taking part in a mass street fight. He liked to have a knife with him wherever he went. A mere ten days before Ben's murder he had been wanted in connection with the stabbing of a 21-year-old man in a drug-related robbery. That case was dropped after the victim refused to give evidence.

The last of this vile group was Michael Alleyne, known as Tigger. He had been freed from a young offenders' institution a few months before murdering Ben and was under the supervision of a youth offending team. The naturally violent dope-smoker – he'd smoked six skunk cannabis joints on the day of the attack – often boasted of his reputation on the street where he would be seen with his pet dog. No lap-dog this: it was, unsurprisingly, a Staffordshire bull terrier he used to intimidate people, setting it on them if he felt like it.

The morning after their cowardly attack, Alleyne and Kika fled to the home of Alleyne's cousin Kellie at Chadwell Heath, Essex, where, while watching TV reports about the murder, they even had the nerve to boast in front of her how many times they had stabbed Ben.

But the net was closing in on the three. Witnesses to the attack were emerging, and when Alleyne and Kika were arrested at Kellie's two days after the murder, despite trying to escape out of the window and over rooftops, their clothes had traces of Ben's blood on them. Braithwaite later turned himself in to police after learning that the Adams family – the crime syndicate notorious in north London – wanted to punish him for committing a crime on their 'turf'.

The three denied involvement in Ben's death, but later began blaming each other after tape-recordings of their incriminating conversations were made. Police were awaiting the result of blood and DNA tests, and engineers had placed bugging devices in the van taking the trio to Highbury Corner Magistrates Court. In one tape the men were heard gleefully talking about how little evidence they felt police had. In another they compared notes about the investigation, laughing and joking as they did.

In one excerpt Kika, whose family were from Angola,

refers to the attack, calling it 'the madness'. He said, using a street language based on American rap music and favoured by so many of his kind: 'See when it happened, yeah. Like boom, it was like a kinda quick ting. Like boom. Went down the road, come back up. Boom, boom. Finished. Boom. Ghost. You get what I'm saying?' He thought the only witnesses to the attack could be 'the people from the houses that were watching on the road. Know what I'm saying?' The three then try to identify the 'snitch' (informant) from their 'endz' (neighbourhood) who had named them as the killers. Meanwhile Kika claimed that 'someone should sort out' a man who ran the council's CCTV cameras that filmed them running from the murder scene.

Braithwaite later told Kika that if he took all the blame for the stabbing he would receive 'Gs' – thousands of pounds. Elsewhere in the conversation Kika wondered if they might be being recorded and said: 'Blood, they sure these tings ain't got no f***ing recording s***, cuz?' Alleyne said: 'Suck your recording.'

Alleyne also wrote to Kellie from his cell, threatening her for 'snitching' on him. One extract from the letter read: 'You will best just hope I don't bust case, cos people will be in trouble and you will never snitch on anyone again.' Another extract said:

You are a let down to the family. You are not my cousin. Believe that. How you gonna give my letters to boyden street [police] *and be snitching on man. You are not real at all, and when will I see you, your mum's still on road, so be careful how you talk. You don't know who I am on road. I'm a boss. When I come out of jail, people from north no hoo I am. I don't need to show you nothing before you tell boyden, you snitch. When the s*** hits the fan you snitch me. I'm a real n****r. I not got time to rite to snitches. All the family know you are a snitch, so if I get found guilty, it's down to you.*

The trial of the three men began at the Old Bailey at the end of April 2009 and was to last over six weeks, with the Kinsella family listening throughout to the painful evidence as witnesses and forensic detail linked the men to the crime.

They were in court when Braithwaite, twenty, Kika, nineteen, and Alleyne, eighteen, were found guilty of Ben's murder and jailed for life all with a minimum of nineteen years to be spent in jail. Amid emotional scenes, the judge, the Common Serjeant of London, Brian Barker, QC, said a 'lifetime of promise' had been ended by 'a brutal, cowardly and totally unjustified attack.'

'The background is depressing and all too familiar in this court. It reflected the futility of carrying and using knives,' he told them. 'Your behaviour generated outrage in all right-minded people and your blind and heartless attack that night defies belief. [Ben] was detaching himself from trouble but he lagged back only to find himself isolated, encircled and attacked by the three of you. He suffered eleven stab wounds and one to the heart was of such force it split his third left rib. No attempt was made to help him in any way and at no point was remorse shown by you in the course of this trial. In my view there is no possible excuse or justification.' The judge said the killers had caused untold anguish to Ben's family and friends.

And the Kinsella family spoke movingly after the emotional scenes in court upon conviction and the sentencing. Amid their grief they pointed out that the minimum sentence handed down to gun murders was thirty years, yet that figure was just fifteen for those who killed with a knife.

Brooke, whose fame as a leading character in one of Britain's most popular programmes had attracted so much publicity to the case, said, 'We've spoken about it as a family and we all feel it wasn't enough. We've been told the judge has certain guidelines he has to follow, but Ben was only sixteen years old and they've got nineteen. The past year has flown by so quickly that those nineteen years they have to do are just going to fly by. As much as the judge tried to give as many years as he could, it's just not enough for us as a family.'

Ben's mother Deborah struggled to hold back the tears as she read an impact statement to the court. Her son's handcuffed killers showed no emotion or even interest as they sat in the dock and listened to her.

'We cry every day for the loss of Ben, we do not sleep like we did before. Nearly a year on, our nights are still filled with nightmares, of our son's last moments and what he went through that fatal night. We as a family will never get over the loss of our Ben, we are just trying to get through it. Our family now face a lifetime of feeling this way.

'No amount of words could ever express the daily pain we feel for the loss of Ben, who went for a good night out and never came home again. Ben had only just finished school, a straight-A student. He had a job and a place in college but he never learnt of the wonderful exam results he had achieved and worked so very hard for. He loved life, he loved living, and he had so much to live for. He knew where he was going and where he wanted to be. He loved nothing more than to make people laugh, he was a fun-loving, happy-go-lucky boy with a heart of gold and would do anything for anyone.

'Ben loved art and wanted to be a graphic designer; he loved his family, cooking, football, music and girls.'

She pointed out the killers 'knew nothing about our Ben, not a hair on his head, a bone in his body, not anything about our wonderful son. They had never met him before or spoken to him, they just cruelly took his life away with knives for no apparent reason.'

She went on, 'We were a big, happy, loving family but now we are one down, one missing. We have had to move house because it broke our hearts to not see Ben in his bedroom, curled up sleeping and safe in his bed.

'We so miss Ben's love and laughter and most of all the boy thing in our family. Ben was our precious son that we cherished and were so immensely proud of. By the way we had brought him up he had values and respected everyone he met. We as a family will never know the man he would have become, the wife he would have met and the children he would have had. This has all now been taken away from us. No one should have to go through or see what we have seen with our son. He died in front of us. We then had to visit him in a morgue, the undertakers and finally to bury him. We can now only visit Ben at a cemetery, our beautiful son who so loved life.'

Perhaps Ben's father George summed up the crisis best in a description that was both achingly personal and yet universally relevant:

'How many families like ours will have to stand outside the Old Bailey to get justice? Our son's only crime was to be the last one to run away from those animals. Knife crime is now sadly embedded in the heart of Great Britain, always running the lives of gangs and feral youths. Parents live in fear until their children are safely home.'

As tragic and moving as those words were, even more frightening was the fear that many other mothers and fathers might be echoing them in the years to come . . .

2

There are some crimes which define the era in which they are committed. Whether it is the swirling Victorian fog of Jack the Ripper's London, the post-war austerity of the acid-bath murderer John Haigh, or the dark side of the sixties, the child-slayers Ian Brady and Myra Hindley, they all become an integral part of the history of their time. The day Philip Lawrence was fatally stabbed outside the school where he was headmaster was such a crime.

It was the dawn of an age where the response to a confrontation was no longer verbal or even rough physicality. Instead it was the quick uncaring thrust of a blade from a feral youth lacking compassion or morality, thinking only of himself and nothing of the havoc caused to those in his way or their loved ones.

It was also a case that was to reverberate for years with the issues it was to raise in relation to the punishment meted out to the attacker.

Of course Philip Lawrence's death was not the first from a knife, but it embodied the period that was about to begin: uncontrollable young men barely out of boyhood, gang culture, schools seen as 'danger zones', and reason and authority dismissed by those who neither understood nor cared for any benefits they might bring.

Philip Lawrence was stabbed outside the gates of St George's Roman Catholic School in Maida Vale, London, on Friday, 8 December 1995, in the most appalling circumstances. He had gone to help a thirteen-year-old pupil who was being attacked by a gang outside the school gates, and yet his reward was to die in a hospital that night after an unsuccessful seven-hour operation to save him.

It was a crime that outraged the nation.

Philip Lawrence grew up in southern Ireland, a bright boy with an interest in literature, whose father was a very good friend of the writer Samuel Beckett from college days and who stayed good friends with him afterwards. As a result the future headmaster was always very interested in Beckett, and went on to read English at Cambridge subsequently teaching at Ealing College, where he met his wife Frances. They moved from London to Wales then Dorset before returning to the capital in the 1980s, where Lawrence took a job at a Brixton comprehensive school, becoming head, before moving to St George's.

Married with four children, he played an active part in his Catholic parish life, and in an interview with a local newspaper, just hours before his death, Mr Lawrence spoke about his passionate commitment to instilling Christian values in his pupils. Referring to violence on the street he said: 'Our biggest worry is life outside the school. We try to make sure the undesirables do not come in.'

It was that desire to spread good that was to lead to his death.

At least twenty-five witnesses were there when he went to the aid of William Njoh, a thirteen-year-old pupil who had been attacked by a dozen-strong gang as he left St George's. The gang, which styled itself on the Triads, was intent on attacking the boy because one of them had been involved in a feud with him. Their young victim was to need hospital treatment for a head injury and a broken finger, but he was to escape lightly compared to the fate which awaited the Ampleforth-educated headmaster who came to his aid.

Learco Chindamo, the son of an Italian gangster, and aged fifteen at the time, saw it as his 'duty' to frighten off pursuers and allow his gang to carry on the beating. His role was dangerous to those who came near him, he was to keep onlookers away. A short distance from the school, Chindamo, by now excited, tense and separated from the rest of his gang, approached the headmaster who asked him what was happening.

The headmaster even adopted what was later termed a 'non-threatening and conciliatory stance with his hands in his pockets to start with'.

Chindamo, dressed in black jacket with its hood up over a baseball cap, said words to the effect of 'What do you want?' and rapidly slapped Philip Lawrence in the face, kicked him on the leg and then, with a knife which appeared suddenly in his hand, stabbed Mr Lawrence once with its ten-inch blade.

Even though he was wearing a vest, shirt, suit and black overcoat, the blow was so hard that it penetrated Mr Lawrence's heavy clothing, entering the left side of the chest, under the armpit. He turned, holding the left side of his chest and practically trotted, then staggered, through the crowd of pupils back towards the school, where he collapsed.

Paramedics were flown to the school where the mortally wounded headmaster was given the last rites before he was taken by ambulance with a police escort to St Mary's Hospital in Paddington; a long operation to save him was unsuccessful and he died at midnight. News of his death quickly spread not just across the nation but around the world and dominated the British media: how could it have happened? What was wrong with a society in which such a crime could be committed.

Father Michael Hopley, who conducted a mass for Mr Lawrence that Sunday, said that Mr Lawrence's wife, Frances, and their children, Maroushka, twenty-one,

Myfanwy, nineteen, Unity, thirteen, and Lucien, eight, were shattered by the murder. 'All we can do at the present time is for the church and friends and neighbours to rally round.'

Father Charis Piccolomini, who had given Mr Lawrence the last rites in the lobby of the school, said, 'I am still trying to make sense of what happened. But one thing that is beginning to speak to me is the wonderful way in which Philip's wife reacted when we learnt of his death. She turned to her children and said: "The first thing we will do when we get home is do what Daddy would have done. We are going to go up to the loft and bring the Christmas tree down. Then we will switch on the lights because that is a symbol of life, and we are celebrating Daddy's life."'

Father Piccolomini, a school governor, went on to praise Mr Lawrence's calm moral authority, saying, 'Philip saw himself as a reconciler and a mediator. Never confrontational, he always reasoned with his students, upholding basic issues of right and wrong.'

That weekend Lucien wrote to Father Christmas asking for his daddy back so that his mummy and sisters 'could stop crying'. The boy's letter was released to the media as the family gathered for mass at their home in Ealing. The words of the youngster encapsulated not only his feelings of bewilderment, but the sorrow felt by anyone of any age at the sudden, violent loss of a loved one.

In his letter, Lucien wrote:

Dear Father Christmas,

I hope you are well and not too cold.

I hope you won't think I am being a nuisance but I have changed my mind as to what I want for Christmas. I wanted to have a telescope but I now want to have my Daddy back because without my Daddy to help I will not be able to see the stars anyway.

I am the only boy in the family now but I am not very big and I need my Daddy to help me stop my Mummy and sisters from crying.

Love from Lucien Lawrence, age 8.

Its simplicity illustrated the suffering more eloquently than a thousand more words ever could.

A week after her husband's death, Frances Lawrence talked of the effect that the slaying had on her life and the impact of knife crime. They were words that were to be echoed in the years to come by other wives whose husbands had been snatched from them needlessly; other men and women who had loved ones taken from them so cruelly and dramatically.

'Of course I am against knives, and of course they should not be readily available, as other weapons should not be readily available. My children are bewildered at the concept of shops selling knives and cannot understand why the government has not clamped down in a very big way.'

Mrs Lawrence, forty-seven at the time, was to maintain

a high profile in the years ahead, and she was one of the first 'victims' to point out that society had to look at the root causes of violence. 'We all have to work together on this . . . A knife is an inanimate object and it needs a human being to invest it with murderous properties. We must not be lulled into thinking that if we get rid of knives we get rid of violence.'

She said she felt that when young people felt unloved and undervalued they 'groped out in the darkness' to find something to fill the void, but often found aggressive behaviour, violence 'and complete disregard for human life'.

Her husband, she said, understood that the purpose of education was to give children options 'so we have to guide them and, for example, help them to appreciate all beauty so there is no room inside them for ugliness'.

He had been fearless but aware of all the dangers outside his school. 'He felt strongly that when things were difficult you should not turn away. Like St George, he knew there were dragons out there, but he felt you must confront them. Philip was my rock, he was my inspiration each day of our life together. I admired him more and loved him more.

'He was fiercely protective of his own children and of children entrusted to his care at school. As parents and teachers he felt we had a duty to try and promote a secure and safe environment where each child's potential could be nurtured.'

By this time she had already received more than 1,000 letters of support, together with flowers and gifts for her children, from all over the world.

And she pointed out, 'Lucien's innocence helped because he can articulate more than any of us our loss . . . I came downstairs and found my daughter looking bemused. Lucien had asked her to post the letter and she was uncertain what to do. As I read the letter, it seemed that Lucien was really speaking on behalf of all of us. At the moment he is just imbued with the whole magic of Christmas, because there is something about Christmas that makes you believe things are going to be all right again . . . Lucien is his father's son. In his own innocence, he says Daddy will be back on Christmas Day, and in a sense we all believe that.

'How does a child or anyone else live in a world of laughter and love one day when the next moment they are confronted by the antithesis of everything they have been brought up to believe as true and good?

'Christmas has always been a very important time for us. This year I can only hope that the routine of Christmas will help the children to get through it and they will find some continuity of opening their Christmas stockings and going to church on Christmas morning. Other than that, I cannot imagine what it will bring. My children have given me any strength I have to go on.'

Chindamo had been tracked down, arrested and

charged with murder by the time of Philip Lawrence's funeral in February 1996. In the lectern where his father used to read the epistle at mass, Lucien stood on a box to reach the microphone to read a prayer he had written for his father. Only the top of his face could be seen by many of the mourners at Ealing Abbey, where his parents had married years before. Many wept as they read copies of the prayer, typed as the boy had written it, complete with spelling mistakes. He wrote:

God in Heaven, help us to think for a minit about
  the time when we all met my daddy.
Help us to think of his kindness.
Not only was he a headmaster but he was my daddy
  too.
I remember the time he bort me something . . . even
  thow it was too expensif.
The time he lernt me to spell words.
How gentle he was.
He played football in the hallway . . . even when he
  had lots of work to do.
Help us to pray that we will meet my daddy again.

The atmosphere was different in September that year when Chindamo appeared at the Old Bailey to face trial for the murder. At that time, due to his age, his name was not publicly revealed and he was referred to as Boy A. Alongside him was Christopher Gan, referred to at that stage as Boy B, and the pair faced conspiracy to commit grievous harm and wounding with intent charges.

The trial laid open, at least in part, the circle of evil that Philip Lawrence had entered that end-of-the-school-week Friday afternoon.

John Bevan, prosecuting, encapsulated the tragedy when he said, 'Part of his job involved looking after the safety of his pupils. It was in looking after one of those pupils that he died.'

He added: 'The first defendant, Boy A [Chindamo], is a leader of a rather different type. Though only a fifteen-year-old he was old enough to lead a gang of youths who deliberately, concertedly and cowardly attacked one of Philip Lawrence's pupils outside the school gates. The gang were armed when Philip Lawrence confronted them peaceably. Boy A, acting with a mixture of bravado and adrenalin, stabbed him in the chest. This represents a tragic waste of life; a genuinely good man killed for the very worst of reasons.'

With Frances Lawrence looking on, Mr Bevan added: 'A fifteen-year-old armed with a knife can be taken to know what it is capable of doing in his hands.'

Mr Bevan said Gan, who was fourteen at the time of the attack, was a gang member who was responsible for the trouble that led up to the tragedy. He had been at the school since before Mr Lawrence joined. The Monday before the murder, Gan had a fight with

William Njoh in the school which produced tension between the pair that 'bubbled all week', culminating in Gan contacting members of his street gang to help him take revenge.

Chindamo and Gan were members of a gang called Wo Sing Wo who 'pretended to be the juvenile equivalent of a Triad gang,' Mr Bevan said. 'They wore black or dark clothes and bandannas or scarves over their faces to represent a uniform and to command respect or to instil fear.'

Gan threatened Njoh, saying the gang would beat him up. Mr Bevan said: 'Boy B [Gan] thought a gang fight was the appropriate response to this troublesome thirteen-year-old boy.' Mr Bevan explained how Gan took a knife to school and gave it to a friend to look after. In the meantime, according to another member of the gang, the eleven-strong group met in a Burger King restaurant in Euston, and travelled by tube to the school for 'home time'.

The leader of the gang, Chindamo, organised them into three groups who walked twenty yards apart as they approached the school. Mr Bevan described it as 'a sort of military operation' in which Njoh was lured a few streets away by Gan where the gang was lying in wait.

The plan went wrong because Njoh sensed danger and when he saw the gang with scarves over their faces he returned to the school where he tried to phone a friend's older brother for help. Andrew Graham, the deputy headmaster, 'sensed all was not well' and called Njoh over. Despite Mr Graham and Mr Lawrence's presence, Gan went up to Njoh and demanded that he should fight.

Shortly afterwards, one member of the gang hit Njoh over the head with an iron bar and the victim ran off dazed and bleeding from the blow.

A short distance from the school, Mr Lawrence was confronted by Chindamo, who had become separated from the rest of his gang. The boy approached and challenged the headmaster. Mr Lawrence may have said to him, 'What is the trouble?' or 'What is going on?' said Mr Bevan, but he added, 'Mr Lawrence adopted a non-threatening and conciliatory stance with his hands in his pockets to start with. Even if he made a grab for the youth's shoulder – that is the most anyone suggests seeing him do – it was no more than was merited in the circumstances.'

Chindamo sneered, 'What do you want?'

Mr Bevan described how the young killer slapped, kicked and stabbed Mr Lawrence. 'The headmaster may never have seen the knife and he appears to have taken no defensive action in advance of the blow.'

Chindamo made the first of his confessions to the slaying when he was asked by one of the crowd why he had done it.

'When someone asked "why", self-preservation took

over and he added, "Shut up, it wasn't my fault, we'd better split up." Everyone appeared shocked at what the youth had said. Of the many eye-witnesses, two knew the youth and saw him do it,' the prosecutor said.

One saw Mr Lawrence, bend over and run back down the road immediately after the punch. He knew the youth and saw what was obviously the knife injury inflicted by him. The second witness, a fourteen-year-old boy who was a former member of the gang, had seen Chindamo 'kicking, punching and then stabbing the head with what looked like a knife with a pointed blade'.

A knife, found near the scene and believed to be the murder weapon, was six and a half inches long with a double-tipped blade which had penetrated nearly three inches.

Njoh told the jury of the events that led up to Mr Lawrence's death and how, four days before the incident, he had fought with Gan in the school corridor after Gan had pushed him on the stairs. Teachers separated them, but they clashed again in the playground and were threatened with being expelled.

Njoh said that Gan told him he was going to 'bring people to deal with me' and he replied, 'Bring them if you want.'

Shortly before 3 p.m. on that fateful day, Njoh said he was approached by Gan who said, as they headed towards a nearby recreation ground, surrounded by friends, that he wanted a fight.

Asked if he recognised the friends, he said, 'I could tell they were Triads. They were lined up against the wall. A few of them were wearing scarves over their faces, a few had on hoods or hats.'

Njoh returned to school to ring a friend for help and while he was there Mr Lawrence asked him what was wrong and told him to go home. But Gan approached him again and said that he wanted to fight. Moments later there was a blow to his head. 'I felt something hit me on the back of my head. I was dizzy. I didn't see it. It was hard. All I saw was black.' Bleeding heavily from wounds that were to need seven stitches, he escaped by running away and sought refuge at a house where the occupant let him in and called an ambulance.

In his defence, Chindamo blamed a friend, who had since left the country, who, he said, had borrowed his coat and baseball cap for the stabbing. Adding, by way of explanation, that he had been 'just boasting' when he later said he was the one who struck the blow.

His denials were of no use. He was found guilty of the murder and Judge Neil Denison, the Common Serjeant of London, ordered him to be detained indefinitely.

The judge told him: 'Philip Lawrence was a good man and an inspirational teacher. He dedicated and devoted his life to providing a future for young people in his care. You took that life and therefore diminished that future. You will be detained during Her Majesty's pleasure.' Chindamo was also found guilty of two other counts concerning the attack on Njoh, and Gan was convicted of conspiring to commit grievous bodily harm and wounding the boy.

And Mrs Lawrence's verdict? 'Learco Chindamo killed my husband and, in doing so, he not only destroyed my family, he also destroyed his own future. My heart goes out to him and his family. I just feel overwhelming sadness that he has not known Philip. Philip might have given time and shown him a better way to live. He might have shown him that the meaning of happiness doesn't lie in the glitzy amusement arcades that he spent his time in.

'I felt a great sadness for him and his lack of values and the lack of anything that shaped his life. People say that some lives are beyond redemption, but I do not believe that. If I did, I would just feel like giving up completely.

'When Learco was in the witness box, he described the minute details of his gang and how it worked. When he was talking about how he paid £3.60 to join, it just broke my heart that any child should find that the way to go forward. The fact that, as my husband was dying, he was playing pool made me feel overwhelming sadness that he knew no more than that, that he thought that was the way to happiness, that he's never been taught or shown anything else.'

She added, 'There was no pleasure to see a young life locked away, but there was a sense of justice. I knew the police had the right man.'

Chindamo was not the only one to be jailed for his actions that shameful Friday afternoon. Gan was later sentenced to be detained for three years and Judge Denison said he accepted that Gan had no direct involvement in the murder and that he deeply and genuinely regretted it. However, he added: 'But it was your actions that started the chain of events that led to that man's death and that is going to remain on your conscience for a very long time.' He recommended that Gan should serve his sentence in a secure accommodation unit.

Details of an eighteen-month reign of terror by the Filipino street gang only became public when reporting restrictions were lifted by an Old Bailey judge.

It emerged that eight members of the gang which attacked Mr Lawrence later raped an Austrian tourist and threw her in a canal to die.

Two of the gang involved in the rape were also in the gang that was hanging around with Learco Chindamo and four others before the husband of the former Director of Public Prosecutions, Barbara Mills, was nearly killed in a street mugging.

The Old Bailey trial came after three gang members tried to get Chindamo cleared by terrorising a crucial prosecution witness; they were detained for a total of nineteen years for attempting to pervert the course of justice. The gang also received a total of eighty-nine years' imprisonment for their various other crimes.

Imprisonment also lay ahead for William Njoh, the boy Philip Lawrence died trying to protect.

Because he had witnessed the killing and given evidence at Chindamo's trial, he was given police protection, while he and his family were moved to a new location. Nevertheless he was sentenced to two years' detention for robbery in 1998 while still in his teens and this was followed by community sentences for burglary and for possession of a bladed weapon and cannabis.

In 2002 he was spotted by police at the Notting Hill carnival smoking cannabis and swigging from a bottle of brandy. He put up a violent struggle with police before eventually being overpowered and handcuffed. They found a loaded Browning pistol, wrapped in a dirty cloth, inside his jacket. He claimed he had been given the gun by an intimidating figure known only as 'Big Foot', but was convicted for possession of a pistol and a bullet in public and two offences of not having a firearms certificate. He was jailed for four and a half years.

Mrs Lawrence said afterwards, 'I think the case reflects not just this desperately sad life of William's, but very much the state we find our society in today. I think it is symptomatic of what has gone wrong in our big estates.' She described Njoh's conviction as the 'single most distressing thing that has happened since Philip died,' and said also, 'I feel a failure because I cannot do more. I feel a sense of responsibility. He is a young man now but, in many ways, he is still a child.'

In the years that have passed since that December afternoon in London, the repercussions of the brave headmaster's death continue.

In 1997 Mr Lawrence was posthumously awarded the Queen's Gallantry Medal, and the Philip Lawrence Awards, established to reward outstanding achievements in good citizenship by young people aged eleven to twenty, were launched nationally the same year to recognise groups 'making a real contribution to their local community and the lives of others; and groups that promote respect and understanding of faiths, culture and communities internationally. The focus is on exemplary activities – examples of young people working together, promoting citizenship and overcoming the difficult situations some young people face.'

By the deed alone that he carried out, Learco Chindamo would have his place in the list of infamous knife-killers, but in its aftermath came a situation that highlighted the rift in society and how those who transgress the laws of civilised behaviour are treated.

In the summer of 2007 a ruling by an Asylum and

Immigration Tribunal that he could not be deported to the country of his birth, Italy, when he finished his prison sentence, caused outrage. Under the terms of the controversial and much-criticised Human Rights Act – and even though the Home Office said he presented 'a present and serious threat' – he was to be allowed to stay in this country.

Frances Lawrence said: 'I am devastated, demoralised. I'm unutterably depressed that the Human Rights Act has failed to encompass the rights of my family to lead a safe, secure and happy life. I feel that I have always been a staunch advocate of the Human Rights Act but there is a missing term in it. It must encompass some responsibility. This isn't just about me and my family. I am not solely thinking of me. I may be a mother but I am a human being as well. I feel I can't fight any more. I feel I can't survive this.'

The ultimate and sickening irony that incensed so many was that as the killer had left Italy when he was so young, he didn't speak the language, and as his relatives lived in this country it would be wrong to deport him. Chindamo, who had wrecked the life of a perfectly innocent family, could not be forced out of the UK because he 'had a right to a family life'.

If there is any truth in the old saying 'the apple never falls far from the tree', it would seem to have been borne out in the case of Learco Chindamo and his father Giuseppe Chindamo. In 2008 the father was jailed for twenty-five years for murdering his former girlfriend and ordered to pay her family almost £100,000 in compensation. The killing took place on the island of Gran Canaria soon after she ended the couple's brief fling and reported the 55-year-old Italian to police for threatening her. Chindamo Senior, nicknamed the Acid Man after he threw sulphuric acid at a previous former girlfriend, ignored a restraining order and began to stalk the 45-year-old woman, finally stabbing her on the steps of a building in the capital, Las Palmas, in front of dozens of horrified passers-by.

In a statement that would make most fathers weep with shame, Giuseppe Chindamo said of his son: 'Everything important in life he learned from me. He looks up to me and respects me.'

3

Kiyan Prince was set to live 'the dream'. He was fifteen and the world lay ahead of him. Not just the 'ordinary' world of education, work, a career, either. His was to be the glamorous existence of a top-flight English footballer; money, fame, adulation, they all lay ahead, beckoning the youngster whose power and energy had earned him the nickname 'the Bullet' on the field.

It was never to be, all because of a flashing blade outside the school gates of the London Academy in Edgware, north London on Thursday, 18 May 2006. Kiyan, who was compared to the teenage prodigy Theo Walcott who later played for England, was a pupil at the school. The boy who stabbed him had been too.

A terse Scotland Yard statement, like so many before and since, could not begin to tell the agony that a violent death brings: 'At approximately 3.35 p.m. a sergeant from a Safer Neighbourhood Team found a youth suffering stab wounds on Kings Drive, Edgware.

The ambulance service attended and the youth was taken to an East London hospital but he was pronounced dead at 5.45 p.m.' Confirming that a murder inquiry had been launched, he said: 'No arrests have been made at this stage. We are keeping an open mind regarding the circumstances.'

The London Academy – with over 1,200 pupils, half from ethnic minorities – had just received a glowing report from Ofsted inspectors. And even though it was in what many would call a deprived area of London it had risen to the top 5 per cent of schools in England for achievement.

A few days after Kiyan's death, a national knife amnesty, the first in a decade since the death of head-master Philip Lawrence, was to come into effect. There had already been a blaze of publicity surrounding it, with the good and the great only too keen to spell out the right message.

It made no difference at all for poor Kiyan.

A spokesman for the academy said: 'Kiyan walked out of school and it seems someone was waiting for him. There did not seem to be any fight or scuffle. It was like he was deliberately targeted. Teachers standing by the gate saw him fall to the ground and it was only when they went to help that they realised he had been stabbed.'

Principal Phil Hearne said children and staff were devastated. 'When I had to announce to people that he was dead, I had very tough senior members of staff in tears. Since then it has been absolute shock. This was a lovely young man. He was looked up to by youngsters here, terribly well respected, an extremely reliable, hard-working, bright young man. He was a natural born leader. We don't know of anybody who would have a grudge against him. There's a real issue of knives in the community. It's our first encounter with knives at a school community, an amazingly tragic outcome from that.'

Counselling was offered to Kiyan's schoolmates to help them cope with their grief. Some sat quietly in corners, others cried. Even those who didn't know him were subdued.

Caretaker QPR manager Gary Waddock told the club website: 'We're all devastated. The club is in mourning at the loss of one of our own. A tragedy like this really puts things in perspective. He was certainly one for the future – a talented lad who really wanted to go on and forge a career in football. It's impossible to express my true thoughts, but I can only offer his family my deepest condolences at this sad time.'

QPR's head of youth, Joe Gallen, said: 'He was an intelligent, smart, good-looking young man with a very bright future in the game and he'll be sorely missed.'

Chairman Gianni Paladini said: 'He was one of our brightest young talents. The way he went about his business was a credit to himself and his family.'

The then Mayor of London, Ken Livingstone, was also affected by the murder: 'The murder of fifteen-year-old Kiyan Prince is a senseless killing and a tragic loss of life. I will be writing to both the Home Secretary and the Lord Chancellor outlining my view that those who choose to carry or use knives should routinely receive the maximum sentence available. The new police teams deployed in every London neighbourhood are targeting those people who think it is clever to use and carry knives. We need to send a very strong message right across the capital that if you commit a crime using a knife in this city, or you are caught with one in your possession, then you will face a very harsh sentence.'

Many others were outraged. Chris Keates, general secretary of teachers' union the NASUWT, said, 'Incidents involving knives and other offensive weapons are extremely rare and schools remain relatively safe havens of peace and security. I have real concerns about the appropriateness, efficacy, or desirability of the suggestion that schools should be able to conduct searches themselves if the intention is that teachers could be required to carry them out. Evidence and experience demonstrates that there is no single measure to tackle pupil indiscipline and improve school security.'

A Home Office spokesman said: 'Sentencing is a matter for the courts but carrying a knife is illegal and won't be tolerated. It can land you with up to four years in prison.

'John Reid [the Home Secretary], like his predecessors, is determined to reduce the devastation caused by knife crime. We will not tolerate the carrying of bladed weapons and are doing everything we can through legislation, enforcement, and community work to prevent it. A national knife amnesty, one of the many tactics the government and police are using to tackle knife crime, is being launched next week.

'Our Violent Crime Reduction Bill increases the age at which a person can be sold a knife from sixteen to eighteen and also provides powers for head teachers to search pupils for weapons.'

There may have been many fine words spoken, but the truth about life on the streets around the school told a different story. Pupils at the school told of how they routinely carried a knife 'because everyone else on the street has got one'. One boy admitted he would use it in a fight 'before the other guy stabs you up'. Even a fourteen-year-old girl, laying flowers for Kiyan near the spot where he was stabbed, said, 'Most boys his age [carry a knife]. They think they have to use it to show how hard they are.'

Although Edgware would hardly be classified as a 'mean streets' area, the school was overshadowed by one of the district's most rundown areas, the Stonecroft estate, identified by the local council as being among the most deprived in the country. The estate, which was awaiting regeneration, was a typical breeding ground for knife-culture with its sprawling ten-storey tower blocks and low-rise flats. The previous year a 24-year-old man had been stabbed to death not far from where Kiyan was killed. The locals said young groups fought to establish their own territories and there were even stories of a Somalian youth spotted wielding a machete.

It was in this setting that the background to Kiyan's death began to emerge. An angry sixteen-year-old had confronted Kiyan and his pal as they left school. In front of twenty youngsters he threatened the smaller boy. 'The Bullet', wearing his football shorts, tried to intervene to help his young friend. Mother of four Sade Howell, forty-six, whose son was a close friend of Kiyan, said: 'He just wanted to break up the fight because he wanted to protect his friend. Kiyan pulled the teenager off and the boy said, "Why did you pull me off?" Then he stabbed him. Kiyan was a really kind person – a hero for many children.'

One pupil said, 'The fight happened round the corner from the school. It was to see who was hardest out of one boy in Year 10 and an older kid. All Kiyan wanted to do was defend his friend. It's sick.'

A fourteen-year-old girl saw Kiyan's friends crying as he held their hands: 'I saw the boy lying on the ground surrounded by teachers, police and pupils. There was blood everywhere, so much I could not believe it. His best friends were talking to him. He was saying: "Don't let me die." They were in tears as they clutched his hands and tried to keep him alive.'

All who knew him were shocked by Kiyan's death.

Sarah Williams, a friend of the family, said: 'Kiyan was only trying to stop a fight between some other kids. He was a really good boy, popular with everyone. He had lovely manners and came from a lovely family.'

Charlie Thomas, fourteen, added: 'He was trying to stop a fight. He was my best friend. He was a good kid who never did anything to anyone. All he wanted to do was play football.'

And close friend Mehdi Hasshim said: 'He was very successful, a very popular boy admired not just by the kids in his year but by those in the years above. He was doing brilliantly in his football and also in his school work and was one of the most talented students here. For him to have a fight at school was totally out of character. He was well built, a big lad, but would never pick a fight – though he would stand up to those who bullied others. He was really in total contrast to the boy who attacked him, who had been expelled and was heading nowhere. Kiyan was somebody with everything and we're all devastated that it has been taken from him.'

Hundreds of tributes were left at the murder spot. One, signed 'Your girl Kristina', read: 'Prince UR 4ever in our hearts. I will remember the last time I saw you and last hug I got from you. Was there ever a time you didn't smile?'

There were so many flowers they had to be moved into the school to enable pupils to get in and out of the building. Inside the building, boxes were being used to keep the countless letters of sympathy that arrived for the dead boy's family.

Pupils, friends and relatives were in tears at the school, embracing each other in their grief or holding hands for comfort. The mourners included Kiyan's older sister, Tanissa, eighteen, who had to be helped as she laid a bunch of flowers wrapped in her brother's school tie outside the school.

One message attached to a bunch of roses read: 'Out of all the people you didn't deserve it. You wouldn't even hurt a fly. You have a heart of gold.'

Another said: 'You were a great boy and you were smart. You could have gone far.' Phil Hearne said the pupils were traumatised by the killing. 'Coming here this morning, I walked through school and talked to as many youngsters as I could and it is very, very quiet. This is a school community that's very exuberant . . . we've got children sitting in corners either in tears or comforting someone in tears. Even youngsters who really wouldn't know Kiyan are upset and being very quiet.

'He was looked up to by youngsters, terribly well respected, and an extremely reliable, hard-working, bright young man.'

A few days after the killing, the teacher reflected on the crises of knives in schools and compared the sense of urgency needed with that shown over the type of food eaten in schools.

'Someone, somewhere has to take the lead on knife crime. But where is that leadership coming from? We are happy to tackle unhealthy eating in schools. But which is the more dangerous – a Turkey Twizzler or a knife?' he asked. 'We have a huge raft of regulations on food – and I don't have an issue with that – but when at least fifty-one people have been stabbed over the weekend nationally then we need to do something about that. How many people have to die before somebody takes this seriously?'

Parents had already given approval for hand-held metal detectors just two weeks before Kiyan died, he said. 'Parents are very much in favour of bringing metal detectors into the school. The next step is to discuss it with staff and students and then after that I would propose it to governors. I personally don't have an issue with it because it is about deterrence. What we have to remember is the knife issue is not peculiar to any one place. This is a national issue. This is not about demonising children.'

He pointed out that his school had until then been relatively free from violent incidents, with just one pupil excluded in the previous twelve months for carrying a knife on the premises. Mr Hearne, forty-six, pointed out that in the USA, there were strategies in place – by presidential decree – to address the issue of safety and security in high schools. He questioned why no such policy existed in the UK. 'Good leadership is about anticipating and I don't see that here. I am not bitter. This is genuine. Where is the leadership to come from?'

Amid the mourning and the launching of the knife amnesty, a plethora of statistics relating to knife crime emerged.

One of them revealed that no one had actually been jailed for selling a knife to an under-sixteen for almost a decade. Home Office statistics showed the last time a prison sentence was handed down for the offence was in 1997 and only nine people were convicted of selling a knife to an under-sixteen in 2004: the lowest figure for three years, the data showed. Six of those escaped with a fine.

Apart from those nine convictions, only one other person had been convicted under the Knives Act 1997, for the offence of unlawful marketing of knives. The figures had actually been given in a Home Office parliamentary written answer at the end of the previous year but had come to light as concern escalated about knife crime.

That late spring bank holiday weekend saw the violence continue. One survey of England's police forces revealed there had been fifty-one stabbings, two of them fatal, over the weekend.

Commenting on the number of knife crimes recorded by the police, Lyn Costello, co-founder of Mothers Against Murder and Aggression, said: 'These figures are just the tip of the iceberg, they are just the serious, reported crimes that have occurred over the bank holiday. We have to do something about this terrifying trend. We need to be arresting people for carrying weapons and giving them tougher sentences. Our children are attacking our children daily.'

Although the figures were chilling, many felt they did not truly reflect the gravity of the situation.

Roger Matthews, professor of criminology at London South Bank University, had carried out a study at a London Accident and Emergency hospital department and found evidence to suggest that only half of stabbings were officially recorded. He said that many of those injured wanted treatment at the scene and did not want to provide names and addresses. 'All the evidence suggests that many, many offences go unrecorded. People always think about how lethal guns are, but many do not work – whereas almost every knife can kill.'

Home Office figures also revealed that seven out of ten youngsters caught carrying knives in school got off with a caution. The previous year, 113 school pupils had been arrested for the offence – which carried a maximum penalty of four years in a young offenders' institution.' But despite a series of school stabbings, eighty-one of them merely received a police caution, which did not count on a criminal record, while twenty were fined. Only twelve ended up in custody.

Margaret Morrissey, of the National Confederation of Parent–Teacher Associations, said a caution was a soft option. 'Unless we put in some kind of really serious sanction then youngsters will disregard it. All that is happening is they are being told not to do it and they are a naughty boy or girl. That will not deter the kind of child who carries a knife.'

Norman Brennan, of the Victims of Crime Trust, said: 'It sends out the wrong message. The clear message should be that if you carry a knife in school, you will be arrested, taken to court, and sent to a young offenders' institute. Letting them off with a caution is a disgrace.'

A national newspaper 'Bin That Knife' campaign showed the scale of the problem. An incredible 89,864 blades were handed in during a five-week period, including cut-throat razors, samurai swords, axes, machetes, meat-cleavers and an 1880s bayonet. Although Tony Melville, of the Association of Chief Police Officers, hailed the campaign a success, saying: 'The amnesty is a step in the right direction and I hope it will prove to be a catalyst in changing the culture of routine knife possession,' other figures revealed a grimmer tale. A survey that showed police in England and Wales had recorded ninety-one serious knife attacks – nineteen of them fatal – during the amnesty, from 24 May to 30 June, and campaigners said more still needed to be done.

Dee Edwards, co-founder of Mothers Against Murder and Aggression, said: 'There need to be education programmes. Nobody ever believed hardened criminals were going to hand their weapons in, but the figures are positive.' Chris Eades, of the Centre for Crime and Justice Studies at King's College London, said: 'This approach confuses the removal of implements with addressing the root causes of knife-carrying.'

Even more figures revealed that muggings at knife-point had risen by 75 per cent in a year, with the government apparently having no idea how to deal with the violence. Statistics published for the first time reveal 42,000 victims suffered the terror of being mugged or robbed by a thug carrying a knife – a staggering increase from 24,000 crimes in 2004/5, according to the Home Office's own British Crime Survey. Another 52,000 victims were confronted by an assailant brandishing a knife – a 55 per cent leap from 33,400 the year before. The number of victims seriously wounded in such incidents leapt 14 per cent from 28,850 to 32,820 last year.

The statistics were obtained by the Centre for Crime and Justice Studies which published a harsh criticism of knife policy: its report stating that the government's response to the growing menace had been 'incoherent' and 'knee-jerk'.

Report author Chris Eades also doubted whether Home Secretary John Reid's plans for tackling the crime-wave would actually work: 'government and the police lack a coherent, evidence based, reasoned strategy for dealing with knife carrying and knife related offences. There is insufficient evidence that a knife amnesty or increasing sentence length for carrying knives will decrease the level of knife use.'

The report said it was highly unlikely that all the knives were taken to police stations by those most likely to use weapons, or who carried them routinely. It added: 'Assuming that there are approximately twenty-two million households in England and Wales, each possessing a single kitchen knife, the amnesty has been success-ful in removing 0.0041 of knives that might be used in crimes. Of course, most households contain more than a single knife and it is barely worth considering the tens of thousands sitting in shops waiting to be purchased.'

Increasing the maximum penalty for carrying a knife from two to four years – the key plank of Mr Reid's plan – was also questioned as the report said those most likely to be involved in knife crime were least likely to consider their actions – making a longer jail term not much of a deterrent.

*

In the middle of this torrent of facts and figures, 750 people attended Kiyan's funeral in north London. Mourners filled every corner of Holloway Seventh-Day Adventist Church and spilled out on to the street as they gathered to celebrate his life. His family and friends carried Kiyan's white coffin, which was covered in a spray of white and pink roses. Many of those at the service wore pink, Kiyan's favourite colour, while floral tributes were in the shapes of footballs, football shirts and the symbol of the school where he was stabbed to death. His father Mark told the congregation that his son was 'not just a prince by name'.

'As a prince, you have to conduct yourself as a prince, deal with people with love, and Kiyan really did. If any of you young people want to look up to somebody and have a role model, use my son, he epitomised success in every area of his life.

'He made some great choices in his fifteen years and I think we can see an example of the great choices he made by the people who have come out today and the effect he has had on people's lives.'

Mr Hearne said Kiyan was an 'almost eccentric' character around the school who was known and loved by all the staff and students. 'He was a beautiful young man, the kind of which in twenty-two years in schools I have never seen before. I hope I will see something like him again, but somehow I think he was such a rarity.' Mr Hearne also said Kiyan was an intelligent, caring young man who had once studied percentages particularly hard because he did not want to be 'cheated' by a future football manager. 'He always smiled and he had such an infectious smile. It was a smile that cheered you up on a miserable day.'

He continued, saying Kiyan was a young man who 'looked out for other people' and added: 'It did not matter to him anyone's age or religion, whether they were black, white or Asian. If they needed help and he thought he could help them, he did his best. He did not tolerate any form of injustice or discrimination.'

Joe Gallen said he signed Kiyan up after watching him play for just five minutes. His attention was first drawn to the sportsman when he heard his name – 'That sounds like a good name, that sounds like a footballer to me' – and even compared Kiyan to England striker Wayne Rooney in the way that he could lift the team just by being present. 'When he came on the pitch he made everyone else play better. He was not a sheep, he was a shepherd and people followed him.'

Some fellow pupils from Kiyan's school wore T-shirts to the funeral with a photograph of him and the phrase 'Kiyan, our lost soldier, rest in peace', and more than a dozen photographs of Kiyan from his early days to his latest teenage exploits were shown on an overhead projector. His coffin was carried away from the church in a procession of more than ten cars for a private family burial service at New Southgate Cemetery.

As that hearse was being driven away a Somali teenager was already in custody, charged with Kiyan's murder. Hannad Hasan had been arrested just thirty-six hours after the knifing, but he had denied murdering the young footballer. There was no dispute that he was the one who swung the blade, he admitted manslaughter, but it was not his intention to murder Kiyan, he said.

The trial of Hasan, who was not publicly named at that stage as he was sixteen, began in October at the Old Bailey where the details of Kiyan's needless death were confirmed. The jury heard that the Somali had sneered at Kiyan: 'Who's laughing? Who's laughing?' before stabbing him through the heart.

He had already pulled out his Swiss army-style knife after scuffling in 'a play fight' with the Queens Park Rangers starlet's pal at their school gates, and Kiyan tried to break it up saying, 'Stop. Stop playing around.' But he and his killer began pushing each other, and Kiyan's friend, referred to in court as Boy A, said: 'He [Hasan] became angry. He said, "If you push me one more time, see what I will do to you." Kiyan was laughing and pushed him again. He [Hasan] put his hand into his right pocket and pulled out a knife and he then put the knife behind his back. When he flicked out the knife I saw it. He grabbed Kiyan's neck. He got him in a headlock with his left arm. He took the knife. He put his arm forward and he stabbed Kiyan. He went for his leg, he went for his chest. He just went for his chest. He was stabbing everywhere. Kiyan made like a painful noise. It was pretty fast. I ran to the scene and I grabbed his hand. I pushed Kiyan to the floor – it was to get him away. I was trying to get him away. I saw Kiyan screaming. He got up and I saw blood. He just came in again and stabbed him again.'

Boy A added that the killer said to him as a teacher approached: 'You can't grass me up. It was just playing.' He went on: 'He was panicking. I picked Kiyan up with another guy. We were walking and Kiyan dropped. He couldn't walk by himself. He said he was fine for the moment but as soon as we let go he went to the ground.'

The teacher on gate duty at the London Academy broke down as she relived finding the popular, 'gorgeous' teenager bleeding on the ground. Liejhe Hernandez told the Old Bailey Kiyan was 'a lovely boy, such a really nice boy, always smiling'. On duty as the school day ended, she saw two boys apparently play-fighting, their arms held out in front of them.

Ms Hernandez said: 'I started to walk across to break it up.' She then saw a boy swung against a car, snapping off a wing mirror and 'knew I had to get help'.

No sooner had she finished calling the deputy head on her mobile, when someone shouted to her: 'Miss, miss, miss.'

She saw a boy on the floor, tending to Kiyan. In tears, the teacher said he was 'holding a shirt over one of Kiyan's arms. I saw it was bleeding. I told him to put pressure on the wound. He lifted Kiyan's shirt and jumper. I saw a little nick on his chest and told him to apply pressure to that. I did not realise how seriously he had been injured at first.'

The fatal stab wound had passed upwards from the lower part of the chest wall into Kiyan's heart. His parents wiped away tears as Mr Nick Hilliard, prosecuting, said there had been no previous trouble between the knife boy and their son.

The killer told police later that the stabbing was an accident. Hasan claimed Kiyan punched him, so he took out the pocket-knife and opened it. When Kiyan punched him again he got him in a headlock and tried 'to leave a little cut' on his arm. Hasan told police Kiyan had started swinging him about and he had 'got him somewhere – I think it was in the chest or something . . . I know I got him in the stomach and the arm.' Although he meant only to scratch, the blade 'went deep in . . . cos I never used a knife before. I thought I stabbed him four times. I did not even know.'

Asked why he was carrying a knife, he replied: 'It was a little toy, it was like a toy I carried every day.'

After his arrest, the Somali teenager told police: 'I am hoping his mum can forgive me. I am terribly sorry. I know how my mum would feel, so I know how his mum would feel as well. He [Kiyan] knows how sorry I am. If he was still alive he would probably have forgiven me, but he is not so I do not know. I hope his family know it was a accident [sic] and not on purpose. I did not do it intentionally.'

He cried as he described to police a play fight that led to Kiyan being stabbed in the heart. The teenager said he had intended to give himself up after the stabbing – but 'I just wanted to talk to my mum before that.'

In an interview after his arrest, he said he had known Kiyan and greeted him when he saw him outside the school.

He was asked by an officer: 'So, it is all about street cred?' and the teenager said, 'Yes.' He told police the stabbing was an accident, saying, 'I did not know I had stabbed him in the heart,' and he had admired Kiyan. They were both good at PE. 'It was my favourite subject. Him and me got to know each other through sport. I was actually surprised that a kid younger than me was better than me in PE activities.'

Hasan declined to give evidence at the trial and eventually the jury failed to agree on a verdict, so a retrial was ordered.

In that second trial Mr Hilliard spoke about the nature of the attack on Kiyan and the type of knife, not a flick-knife, used: 'You have to open the blade out yourself. It requires a very deliberate action. There came a time when the defendant decided to take out his knife and he chose to open the blade attachment. Well, that's not a play fight, is it? It had become deadly serious, literally, as it turned out. Kiyan did push him again and the defendant had the knife out. Other children were there witnessing this as they came out of school. The defendant may have thought he was losing face in front of them.'

That second trial had to be abandoned because of what was termed an 'incident' involving one of the jurors away from the court when Kiyan's father spoke with a juror, and so a third, and final, trial began in mid-summer 2007 which eventually ended with Hasan being found guilty of murder.

Hasan didn't give evidence in any of his trials and was therefore never cross-examined about the events that day or what had led up to them, so it was only after the guilty verdict that full details of his life – and evil character – emerged.

Hasan had burst one girl pupil's eardrum in a confrontation, punched others, thrown chairs and – less than a week before he killed Kiyan – was excluded from his school after threatening to smash or kick someone's face in and urinating in front of a female teacher and threatening another teacher.

And in an incident on a bus, he threatened to stab a girl during a trivial row over a seat less than two weeks before Kiyan's death, asking his friends to give him a knife, saying he was going to shank (stab) her. He also slapped her, although these frightening incidents were disputed by his defence team.

During his trial, but in the absence of the jury, the court heard that the girl's father had been appalled by the threat to cut her and went to see the defendant at his home and obtained an apology – although it appeared from his statement the apology was for hitting her.

The bus incident witnesses came forward to testify as to the nature of the young Somali after they learnt of Kiyan's killing, but the jury were never told of his previous violent outbursts.

A 'catastrophic' failure by the prosecution to give the defence sufficient notice they wanted to bring evidence of the alleged bus incidents meant it was excluded from the trial and legal procedures also precluded his full school record being presented to the jury.

Hasan had come to Britain from Somalia in 2001 with his refugee mother and he became obsessed with Somalian gang culture. But the gangs couldn't help him as he stood, head bowed, to be sentenced to life imprisonment by Judge Paul Worsley.

The judge said, 'This is yet another case of a wholly unprovoked stabbing in a public place, by a person who produced a knife and plunged it into the heart of their unarmed victim.' He added: 'Taking the life of another is always a terrible thing, taking the life of a talented, popular fifteen-year-old schoolboy who was known to you and who had done you no wrong and had everything to live for defies description. You have deprived his family and school friends of a role model.

'Whether or not you were jealous of Kiyan Prince's popularity and sporting achievements, I'm satisfied you stabbed him in order to show off to your friends and seek to show superiority over a boy you thought was stronger and fitter than you. You not only destroyed his life but ruined the lives of those near him.'

In mitigation, Hasan's defence counsel George Carter-Stephenson, QC, said the killing was 'not a planned or premeditated attack, it was very much a spontaneous event that occurred out of what must be momentary anger and was instantly regretted'.

But the judge said Hasan's actions showed 'little genuine remorse' and sentenced him to a minimum of thirteen years for his crime. A deportation order was also made.

As always, however, the grieving had to be done by those who were left behind; Kiyan's mother Tracy Cumberbatch and his father, former boxer Mark Prince, who had both sat through every day of the three trials, put their feelings into words, not only in their impact statements but in reflective conversations later.

Ironically Tracy had moved to the area after separating from Kiyan's father because she felt it was a safer place to bring up their children than Tottenham where she had previously lived.

'Kiyan was just two and a half and his sister Tanissa was a little older. I just felt they would have better opportunities if we moved to Edgware, like better schools. I wanted a fresh start and the break-up gave us a chance for that. It's so sad he died where we thought his life would be improved.'

She remained close friends with Kiyan's father, explaining: 'We both decided how we wanted to bring up our children. Kiyan had a stable upbringing. Just because the parents are not together, it doesn't mean you change the way you bring up your kids. We disciplined him and loved him and taught him right from wrong. Kiyan was my soulmate. He was a pleasure to know and bring up. He was very loving and fair.'

Youth worker Mark said: 'There's no doubt this guy was jealous of my son. According to witnesses, as soon as Kiyan arrived on the scene Hasan's attitude changed. He had been play-fighting with Kiyan's friend, but the moment he saw Kiyan, he went for his knife. In police interviews, he spoke repeatedly about how my son and his friend were bigger than him and how they had street cred. I believe over a number of months Hasan had become obsessed because Kiyan was more popular. But that deep-rooted envy was allowed to grow inside him, eating him out, unchecked.'

Tracy said Kiyan would have been unaware of Hasan's

jealousy. 'He couldn't understand why people would want to hurt him. We had to sit him down and explain that no matter how you live your life, there are people in this world who will do anything to bring you down. Sadly, that came true. Hasan said he only meant to scratch Kiyan, not kill him. So why did he, by his own admission, swing at him four times with a knife? He is a coward. He waited until Kiyan was on the ground before aiming the final blow.

'We have nothing to say to him or his family. We wanted him to stand up in court and give his account but he didn't. It was sad to see him walking past us and waving and joking with his family in the public gallery. It's no joke.'

Both parents said Hasan should never be released and believe the justice system is tilted too far in favour of young thugs. Tracy said: 'Life should mean life – until you die in prison. Not ten or twelve years and you're out after good behaviour. We are too soft on young offenders in this country. No matter what sentence he gets he will still come out. He is still alive. His mum will have her son but I don't have mine.'

Mark added: 'We are pleased justice has been done. We wanted the jury to understand this was a case of murder and not manslaughter and they did.'

Both parents had gone to the hospital on the day Kiyan died and Mark was so overcome with grief he punched holes in the hospital walls in his agony.

Mark identified his son, but said, 'It was like some-one was shoving their fist into my chest and pulling my heart out.'

Tracy said: 'He looked like he was sleeping. I kissed him on the lips. I remember he never used to like me doing that – me being all mummy towards him. I couldn't let go of him. I told him I'd done everything I could as a mum but couldn't protect him. I remember he was still very warm. It was our last goodbye. Hasan will never understand the pain we went through that night.'

But Kiyan left a legacy in the shape of the Kiyan Prince Foundation, set up by his parents with the aim of going into schools, youth centres and 'pretty much anywhere' they could to help young people. Among the Foundation's aims were to educate young people about the positive effects of good communication and social skills and to raise awareness of the impact young untimely deaths have on families and friends. 'Our Mission is to tackle our rising violent youth culture head on and reduce unnecessary suffering to parents, the community and to raise young people's aspirations to reach their full potential and value their lives and the lives of others,' they said.

And in a moving message they told the world of their aims and how something good could come out of some-thing so bad.

'We hope we can change lives and may even help to

save them. Unfortunately there wasn't a campaign like this to save my son Kiyan. He was taken from us last year by another victim of so-called "Gang Culture".

'Our son, our boy was a unique human being. When he died, a part of us died too. Kiyan was not in a gang, he didn't carry weapons. It's true he loved his rap and his street fashion, in fact he loved all kinds of different music. One thing we know is that he didn't mess with drugs and he didn't commit street crimes or bully other people. Kiyan was nothing but a normal, typical teenager who lived his life to the full. Every parent likes to think that of their child but we had reason to. Kiyan was popular at school among pupils and staff. The turn out at his funeral was evidence of that. He worked hard at his subjects but his true passion was his sport. Kiyan played for the Queen's Park Rangers Youth Team. He was an outstanding footballer dubbed the next Beckham and a future England international. He was a prolific goal-scorer who brought the best out of his teammates. On May the 18th 2006 Kiyan's dreams . . . his popular life . . . his destiny . . . his family . . . were all destroyed with a quick sharp stab into his heart. His life was taken by a teenager armed with a simple knife.

'Think about those words for one moment. His life in a brief second taken from him by a teenager with a knife. It's a crime that should never happen, but it does, far too often on our streets, in our playgrounds, clubs, swimming pools, shops and parks. Nowhere is it safe, it seems, and no child, black or white, is excluded from this problem. Gang culture or whatever you want to blame for this epidemic is killing our precious children almost on a weekly basis. We hope and pray that Kiyan's death can inspire and change the misguided youth on our streets.

'We have decided to launch the Kiyan Prince Foundation to help and support a growing number of projects and individuals to help and deter our children from a gang culture and to give them a sense of purpose in life.

'We cannot bring our son Kiyan back, but we can, with your help and love, keep his memory alive.'

4

It was a question so sickening in its implications and underlying threat that even to repeat it brings a feeling of revulsion to any civilised person.

Dean Curtis, a teenager with violence on his mind, posed it to young father Kevin Johnson.

He asked him, 'Do you want to meet Mr Stanley?' The 'Mr Stanley' in question was the pocket-size knife with a razor-sharp blade that can be slipped back into its covering metal case. It bears the name of the American tool-making company who mass-produce it, and it is beloved of carpet-fitters and handymen worldwide for the precise edge it gives when cutting.

It is also deadly in the wrong pair of hands and Dean Curtis was most definitely the wrong pair of hands. Moments after making the threat to Kevin, the 22-year-old dad was dead, a bloody victim of 'Mr Stanley'.

And what had he done that 'deserved' such a fate? What was the 'crime' that prompted the attack with the knife? Kevin Johnson simply asked Curtis and his two pals, who had all been drinking, to keep quiet as the noise they were making outside his house late at night might wake his baby son.

For that he died. And were the trio responsible sickened by their act? Not in the slightest. They left Kevin, bloodstained from the three wounds from the knife, collapsing a few feet from his front door and ran off in what was later described as 'a triumphant mood'. Within minutes they had stabbed another man.

Kevin Johnson was a fit, muscular man who lived with his fiancée Adele Brett, twenty-six, their six-month-old son Chaise and her seven-year-old son from a previous relationship. Kevin and Adele had been out for the evening with friends, and at 11.30 p.m. on Saturday, 19 May 2007, they returned to the three-bedroom council semi-detached they had only recently moved into on the massive Pennywell estate in Sunderland. Soon afterwards neighbour Marsha Newby was woken by raised voices and saw Mr Johnson at his bedroom window shouting at a man outside his house. A short time later she heard the noise of Kevin's front door being opened.

The gang had provoked him into coming outside for a fight and were beckoning with their hands, walking away from Kevin, clearly enticing him to come towards them. All three were closing in on Kevin. One of them was moving his arms across his chest and Kevin was dodging out of the way. Two got closer to Kevin – as he backed away he appeared to stumble and fall to the floor. He got back up and one of the men, the one furthest away, threw a rock or brick at him.

Then Kevin realised he had been knifed and said, 'You couldn't fight with your hands. You've stabbed me,' and he collapsed at a low wall struggling for breath.

Adele found him slumped against the wall outside and dialled 999 telling the operator: 'I think my boyfriend has just been stabbed. I think he has been stabbed. He's fallen over a wall. Three boys have come round the corner causing trouble. He went outside to try to stop them.'

A neighbour said: 'Kevin came out and asked them to stop making a noise because they were keeping the baby awake. He was not confrontational and there was no history with this group as far as we are aware. But they still killed him. He didn't stand a chance.'

An ambulance arrived ten minutes later and although Kevin was still breathing he was fading fast so the paramedics could barely find a pulse. His fiancée followed in a police car, but forty minutes after he arrived at Sunderland Royal Hospital he was pronounced dead.

As their victim's life ebbed away Curtis and his pals Tony Hawkes, who was seventeen, and Jordan Towers, sixteen, damaged two cars and bragged to one another about the stabbing. Then they approached another man, Jamie Thompson, who was on his way to an all-night garage when he was unlucky to encounter the trio in nearby Grindon.

One of the three approached him: 'He asked me for a cigarette. I didn't have any. The other two crossed over to me. They were in my face and the first one was just behind those two. They came up to me and one of them said "Are you Jamie" and I said yes. They wanted to fight me. They were saying they wanted to fight me. I thought they would hit me. I didn't say anything else. I tried to walk back but they came further up to me and I stopped. That's when I got stabbed. He did it quick. He pulled it out of his coat. I was shocked. I turned around and ran and when I looked back they were standing laughing, shouting. I went to a house for an ambulance.' The entire incident lasted just two or three minutes and Mr Thompson was taken to hospital for treatment for the stab wounds to his chest.

He, at least, managed to survive the attack, unlike demolition worker Kevin who had been stabbed once through the arm, once in the back and once in the heart. He also had bruising around his mouth from what could have been a punch and there was an indentation in his clothing from what could have been a knuckleduster. A blood-stained 'duster' was later found 100 yards away.

The three attackers, who had all been drinking, spent the next few hours wandering the streets during which time they dumped their bloodstained clothes and stole replacements from washing-lines. One of them, Hawkes, took a call from his mother and said to her: 'I've just stabbed someone.'

Curtis went to a friend's house where he boasted about the killing. He said he had been involved in a fight with a man and claimed to have punched and kicked him before asking the grotesque phrase: 'Do you want to meet Mr Stanley?' A red-handled Stanley knife was later found by police at his grandmother's home.

The death of a young man such as Kevin has a devastating effect on those around him. Fiancée Adele Brett was one such victim.

Like many who have suffered a sudden loss, even after his death she expected him to walk through the door at any moment. 'Kevin never harmed anyone in his life. He died because he tried to keep peace and quiet near his own home. I don't know what is happening in this country when you are not safe on your own front doorstep. It is only my children who keep me going – I have to struggle on for their sake. My life and the lives of the whole family have been devastated by Kevin's death. It is a struggle to eat, to sleep and to watch telly or just to listen to music. Everything brings back just how empty life is without Kevin. It makes me very sad and angry that he was robbed of all the things he was looking forward to as a father – Chaise's first steps, his first day at school and taking him to his first football match.

'Sometimes I wonder why we bring kids into this world. It can be a terrible place to live. When he is old enough to understand, I will tell Chaise the truth about what happened to Kevin and let him know the kind of person his dad was. Kevin was the most brilliant dad. He was so proud of our son that nothing was any trouble to him. He called him My Little Smurf because he was so small, yet perfect. He bathed him, played with him and got up in the night to take his turn at the feeds. To see the love in his eyes was wonderful.'

Kevin proposed to Adele on Christmas Eve and although they hadn't set a date they were saving up for their 'modest affair' wedding. They were even talking about having another child.

'Sometimes when I cook dinner I find myself putting out a pudding for Kevin as well as me and the boys and I get very upset. I can still see and hear him outside the house on match days shouting with joy at the top of his voice when Sunderland scored. It was so loud that sometimes Chaise would cry. I feel Kevin's presence everywhere in the house. On the day before he died he left a packet of crisps on the bedside table. I still can't bring myself to move it.'

Kevin had been a massive Sunderland fan and had bought a season ticket for the coming season to celebrate his side entering the Premiership. At Kevin's funeral, friends, colleagues and family wore Sunderland football shirts. Little Chaise wore a tiny soccer shirt with 'No. 1 Dada' on it – 'Dada' was the first word the child ever spoke. A horse-drawn carriage, pulled by two seventeen-hand chestnut-brown horses with red and white plumes headed the procession, and inside the black carriage a red and white coffin was draped with a flag emblazoned with the football club's badge, itself surrounded by flowers, spelling out 'Kev'.

His older brother Darren wrote in one message: 'To the funniest bloke I've ever met. Thanks bro for all the days I had with you. I am really going to miss our days playing pool in Rileys, I bet you got sick of getting your bot kicked eh? I will also miss every Saturday texting each other when the mighty SAFC [Sunderland] were playing. I love you Kev, I never said it often, but I know you knew. I hope our nana is holding your hand in the place where you came from.

'Just thinking of you releases the hurt and pain. By Heaven's gate Kev we will meet again.'

Adele added: 'These three people have taken away my life, my future children and my wedding day. We never even had the chance to have a family holiday.

'Kev only got to see his son's first seven months. He will never see his son's first tooth, his first haircut or his first day of school. He'll never be able to play football with him or take him to a match.

'Chaise will never have his own memories of his dad, just other people's.

'People keep telling me it will get easier over time but they are wrong – it gets harder. You just learn to put a public face on it better. I'm counting the weeks since I saw him last. I miss him so much.

'I hope these three people realise what pain and suffering they have caused.'

Darren also wrote a poem in his memory that was printed in the local newspaper:

A baby boy was born with stunning blue eyes.
We named him Kevin an angel in disguise.
A loving adorable son and a wonderful brother.
We love you so much, love like no other.
His spirit was special, full of life.
He left us a son and a soon to be wife.
His legacy lives on in his son Chaise.
With his cheeky grin and lovable face.
On my arm forever, your name will be worn.
My heart is broken, forever torn.
The angels arrived on that fateful night.
To make sure my brother spread his wings in flight.
You arrived in heaven to our Nana's embrace.
Have fun with the angels in your final resting place.
Never look back Kevin, stay in the light.
I will see your face in my dreams at night.
Visit me often bro, I will be fine.
I will cherish my memories of you until the end of time.
It's not the same without you, my heart is torn.

KNIFE CRIME

I am so glad little brother that you were born.
Someone please tell me why my brother was killed.
Why did there have to be so much blood spilled.
Empty inside from the loss and the pain.
By heaven's gate Kevin, we will meet again.

Written by Darren for an angel in disguise,
my little brother. R.I.P.

After the funeral some of Kevin's ashes were buried under a corner flag at the team's Stadium of Light ground. When Adele went to one home game she said that she could even 'feel Kevin's presence'.

And what of Dean Curtis, the young man who enjoyed making remarks about 'Mr Stanley'?

When he and his two friends appeared at Newcastle Crown Court in October that year, and all denied murder and wounding with intent, he maintained that he was 'an innocent bystander'. He gave evidence the day before Chaise's first birthday and said the three of them had met at a friend's house where he had drunk some vodka and beer before they all broke into a shed at a disused property nearby. Curtis said he found a Stanley knife inside the shed, which he had put into his pocket because one of his friends had suggested it would be a good tool to cut up plastic bottles, which they would use to smoke cannabis.

He said: 'I put the knife in my pocket and forgot all about it.' Later that night, after downing more vodka, the three began walking down the road where Kevin lived. Tony Hawkes began to let car tyres down and smashed a car wing mirror.

Kevin looked out at the group through the blinds of a window at his home, and Hawkes reacted aggressively to this, Curtis said.

'We were walking past and someone was looking out of his blinds. He [Hawkes] said, "What is that idiot looking at?" I didn't say anything, I just said "Haway, we'll walk on." He was shouting at the gadgy to come downstairs. Kevin came out of the house and said "Be quiet" and he [Hawkes] started to give him loads of abuse and stuff like that. They started fighting, him and Kevin, they were punching each other, stuff like that. I ran over because I saw Kevin was a big size and I thought he [Hawkes] is drunk, he is always cheeky and is going to end up getting knacked. I feared for him so I ran over and he was getting knacked by the time I ran over. He stumbled backwards and Kevin was still punching. I got to where they were fighting and Kevin seemed to move back and dived on me. I don't know if it was just to keep himself up or to stop me. He had me around me waist at first, his hands around my waist. He [Hawkes] ran over and was trying to get him off me then I heard Kevin make a noise. I was shaking my leg saying, "Get off me." He approached from behind. I didn't see what he did but Kevin made a noise, like he was getting stabbed in the back or something. Kevin slid down my legs.'

Curtis said Towers then threw a brick towards Kevin. He added: 'I just walked away. Kevin pulled his top up. He was getting off the ground. He was saying, "You've stabbed me. You've stabbed me. You couldn't fight me with your hands. You've stabbed me." I know he said he had got stabbed but he was walking away so I thought he was all right.'

He added: 'I wish I had run off. I wish I had never gone out with him.'

Curtis said that as he and his pals walked away Hawkes put something that looked like a knife in his trousers. Hawkes then confessed he had stabbed Kevin in the chest. He also maintained he had nothing to do with the attack on Jamie Thompson just moments later, although he was there when the stabbing must have happened.

Robert Woodcock, prosecuting, said that all three had played their part in the killing of Mr Johnson. Three weeks later, in his closing statement to the jury, he said easy access to knives was unavoidable '. . . because you will have paid over recent years a lot of attention to media hype surrounding the prevalence of knife crime. You will have heard and read how succeeding governments have promised to stamp down on knife crime. Though you are bound to wonder what on earth any government or organisation can do when individuals, such as these three defendants, need only plunder into their mothers' kitchens for a perfectly innocent kitchen knife to arm themselves as they wander aimlessly, or perhaps not so aimlessly, around the housing estates of Sunderland at night time.'

The court had heard all three were carrying knives and, even if it was impossible to say who delivered the fatal blow, all three were on a 'joint enterprise'. Curtis and Hawkes blamed each other, while Towers did not give evidence.

After four hours of deliberation the jury found the trio guilty of all charges, and as Hawkes was led away to his cell he turned to his supporters in the public gallery and said one word: 'Easy.'

When he sentenced the three some weeks later, Judge David Hodson jailed Curtis for life with a minimum term of seventeen years, Hawkes was detained at Her Majesty's pleasure with a minimum term of sixteen years and Towers was also detained at Her Majesty's pleasure with a minimum term of thirteen years.

The judge spoke, as had many judges before and since, of the cowardly culture in the country, saying, 'There's nothing macho in carrying knives – it's the mark of a coward. This case illustrates yet again the sheer stupidity and obvious inherent danger of young men carrying knives. It's all too easy, particularly when fuelled up with drink, to use them. The whole country is painfully aware of the frequency with which knives are carried and used; often, as in this case, there are terrible consequences for the victim and their family. The sooner that people in general, and in particular boys and young men, realise the risks they are running and stop carrying such weapons, the better.'

Detective Chief Inspector Roger Ford said later: 'We could quite easily have been looking at a double murder. It is just luck the attack on the second victim did not cause a life-threatening injury.

'We've been able to secure these convictions through a combination of good detective work, the support of the CPS and the Forensic Science Service.

'Although the weapon used was never recovered, the DNA on the coat of the second victim matched that of Kevin Johnson, showing the same knife was used in both attacks. In all probability the knife used was a small kitchen knife. This was a brutal and cowardly murder. Throughout this investigation, though, our thoughts have been with the family of Kevin Johnson who have acted with great dignity since day one. They have been left traumatised by the events of that night and I know Kevin's partner Adele is devastated that their son Chaise will never really know his father and Kevin will not see his son grow up and all those moments which make being a parent so special.'

Adele – who had changed her surname by deed poll to Johnson by this time – said: 'I hate them with a vengeance. All I feel is pure hatred for what they did. I have no idea why people go out carrying knives. It is not being a big man, it is being a coward.'

After sentencing, Kevin's father John Johnson said that although he was pleased with the length of the sentences, he believed, as did many other families who lost a loved one to a knife attack, that a life sentence should mean life.

Speaking at the foot of the steps outside Newcastle Crown Court, with his wife Kathleen and more than a dozen family members, he said: 'They got seventeen, sixteen and thirteen years, which is a long time, but I want life to mean life. Kevin is not coming back and they should not come back. The judge said a lot of good things and they got more than we expected, but like I say, life to me should mean life and they should come out of prison in a box. I would say to people "do not be a hero." It's not safe to stand up for yourself any more.'

Mr Johnson also launched Enough is Enough, a campaign that he hoped would shake up the current laws and make sure 'life is life' when murderers are given a life sentence.

He said: 'I want to see the law changed so that life means life imprisonment for people that kill. This will be the biggest deterrent and might make people think twice before putting a knife in their pocket.

'If someone's going to carry a knife round with them it means they are going to use it and now there is no deterrent in place.

'I am doing this because I feel anger and rage and I wanted to channel it into something purposeful,' he added. 'But this is something that should have happened years ago.'

Mr Johnson also said: 'It's becoming a massive problem and it causes the victims' families huge amounts of grief.

'Knife crime is starting to grip the area more and more and something needs to be done fast. Kevin was such a hard-working lad who loved his family. How many more people have to die before something is done?'

As part of his campaign, Mr Johnson and other families affected by knife crime presented a 35,000-signature petition at Downing Street calling for tougher sentences in cases involving knives.

And he also wrote a remarkable open letter to the three killers:

I am the father of Kevin Johnson, the young man whose life you took without a second thought. Kevin was a much-loved son to me and his mother Kath. We'd brought him up as part of a decent, hard-working family and we were very proud of him. He was a lively, fun-loving little boy when he was growing up – mad on sport, especially football.

He played football for his school for one season and always supported Sunderland.

I can still picture him jumping up and down and yelling when he listened to the match on the radio and they scored.

He also loved hip-hop music. I was always into the Beatles and the Stones but for Kevin it was always boom, boom, boom – the noisier the better. Sometimes one of his favourite songs – like 'Ruby' by the Kaiser Chiefs – comes on the radio and it is enough to start the tears.

He was a devoted dad to his new son Chaise and his seven-year-old stepson Trey. His fiancée Adele was the love of his life. She is now a broken woman.

They should have been man and wife by now, with another child on the way. That was their dream.

Instead Adele cannot get over the terrible events that you caused, and then gloated over without a shred of remorse . . . You are responsible for robbing our family of a future so full of promise. Chaise and Trey know who their dad is – there are photos of him all over the house and we talk about him all the time.

But how can that make up for him not being there to watch over them and keep them safe? You will still be in your late 20s or early 30s when you get out of prison, young men with the rest of your lives to look

*forward to. You have made sure Kevin never got past
the age of 22.*

*We spent his 23rd birthday burying his ashes at
the Sunderland football ground where he should have
been cheering the team on with his sons in years to
come . . .*

*If any good at all can come from the evil that you
did it is that it will force changes in the law. People
caught carrying knives MUST be given the four years
proposed for the offence. Changes may come too late
for us. But others like you may not be so keen to stick
a knife into somebody if they knew that a life behind
bars would be the certain result.*

There was one final twist in the case of Kevin Johnson.

In 2009, after being turned down on two previous
occasions by the Criminal Injuries Compensation
Authority, his family appealed again for compensation.
A hearing was held in private and the family was
supported in their bid by Northumbria police. After an
hour-long hearing the panel of three ruled that the
Johnsons were entitled to compensation and awarded
them a 50 per cent payout of £5,500 – half of what
they could have won because Kevin had left his house
and confronted the yobs.

Self-employed taxi driver John said: 'They've turned
us down twice and why did they do that if they have

given [compensation] to us on the third attempt in front of the tribunal? Most families will get that first letter and say "Oh well, that's it." Is that a ploy by the government to curtail monies? Not everyone's got the willpower that I've had.'

He also said: 'A criminal can go inside and get beat up and claim thousands. They have got previous convictions as long as your arm and if Kevin had a minor infringement he would have been turned down for that. He didn't.

'He left the safety of his house, so what they are more or less saying is let the scum rule the streets and don't go out to them and don't stand up to them. You've got to call the police. I reckon most people would have done what Kevin did. When there's rowdy behaviour outside your house it's just human nature to go out.

'Hindsight is a lovely thing. If he thought he was going to get murdered he wouldn't have gone out, but you don't think of them things.

'It's not really the money, it's the way they blamed Kevin. Muddying his name and his character. That's what rankled with us.

'No amount of money you could give us would ever be enough for Kevin. They have got to put a price on it and £11,000 is the price that they put ... We're the victims all the time and we'll be the victims until we die. The whole emphasis is on the criminals and they get everything they want inside.

'If Kevin had a criminal record we would not have been able to make a claim at all. But he never did. They had convictions as long as your arm but it's called human rights.

'It's all wrong.'

5

Knives kill in the most mundane of places.

Stabbings and the indiscriminate use of a blade are often associated with dark streets, bar brawls or inner-city gang wars.

Yet the thrust of steel in the midst of everyday life can bring death where it is least expected. Nowhere is safe any more.

Certainly not the 10.10 a.m. Virgin train from Glasgow to Paignton in Devon on Saturday, 27 May 2006. As it passed through some of the most beautiful countryside in the land, the express was about to become the scene of one of the most indiscriminate acts of knife savagery that has taken place in this country, even in a Britain gone mad.

On board was Thomas Grant, a young man who had his life ahead of him. He'd been a boarder at the £20,000 a year Oakham School in Rutland where he'd captained the school's football team and was also the leading cadet in the cadet force. Thomas left with top grades in history, politics and French at A level, and an A in his German AS level; in recognition of his all-round effort, the school awarded him its prestigious W.W. Holman prize for the pupil with the most promise, endeavour and achievement.

He had just finished the first year of a history and Arabic degree at St Andrews, the 600-year-old university – north of Edinburgh so popular with public-school pupils – including Prince William – it was often called 'England's most northern university'. Like the Prince, Thomas hoped to go to Sandhurst after university.

The only reason nineteen-year-old Thomas, a Squadron Leader's son, was on that particular West Coast Main Line train that fateful day was that it was one of the trains that allowed him to take his bicycle on board.

He had originally planned to spend a fortnight at an officer training camp in the Lake District, organised by Tayforth Universities Officer Training Corps, of which he was a respected member, but had pulled out at the last minute on account of a knee injury. Instead, he was off home to Churchdown, Gloucestershire. His fellow cadets would weep when the news of what happened next was broken to them the following day by their commanding officer.

Thomas had to change trains at Carlisle, and it was while he was standing on the platform that his life crossed with that of another Thomas: Thomas Wood.

Shaven-headed Wood had just been released from prison on 11 April after serving just half of a six-month burglary sentence. He was living with his girlfriend, Sarah Chadwick, in Skelmersdale, a designated new town just twelve miles north of Liverpool and a social universe away from public schools, universities and a future life of achievement. The only thing the two Thomases had in common, apart from their names, was that they both supported Liverpool FC – and, of course, that they were to board the same train.

In the weeks between his release and that train journey, Wood and Sarah Chadwick developed a stormy relationship and often argued. The week before 27 May they went to stay with an aunt of Chadwick's, Sarah Dunsheath, in west Cumbria. While they were there, a few days before the fateful train journey, Wood punched Chadwick hard in the stomach during an argument, despite believing she was pregnant by him. He was that sort of guy.

Wood threatened to kill her when she warned him she would call the police over his attacks, and he even threatened to throw her through a window. It wasn't just human beings who were a target for this habitual cannabis smoker: in one of his rages he even punched and kicked a bus shelter in an attempt to demolish it.

Wood, Chadwick and Ms Dunsheath and her children were travelling to Skelmersdale on that Saturday, and, sulking, Wood tore up his ticket after yet another row. When Chadwick warned him he would be thrown off the train if a ticket collector was on board, he said: 'No, I won't, because I'll stab him.'

At Carlisle they were standing on the same platform as doomed Thomas Grant, and Chadwick was talking to one of the others about what she planned to have for her tea that evening. Wood, typically, said he would steal some food for her. Thomas Grant heard this remark, turned and looked at the group and then turned his head away.

Wood's response to this was simple. He looked at him and said, 'What the f*** are you looking at? I'll stab you in a minute.'

It was a hate-filled remark from a twisted young man that would have been grotesque enough if it had been an idle threat. Sadly it wasn't. It was a statement of intent from a man with an uncontrollable violent streak. Also, inside his pocket was a four-inch kitchen knife he had taken from Ms Dunsheath's house.

Thomas Grant got on the crowded train and sat near his bicycle, which he stowed in a compartment nearby. Wood, the two women and children sat at the other end of the same packed carriage. Yet again there was a row between Wood and the women about tickets and Wood made Chadwick cry before beginning to walk up and down the corridor as though he were stalking an unseen prey.

Passenger Paul Cunningham recalled: 'It was as if he

was looking for trouble and looking for eye contact. I didn't want to have eye contact with this person as I thought he was trouble.'

A few minutes later, as the train thundered past the village of Tebay, Wood returned to the carriage through the sliding door carrying a knife in his hand. He looked to his left at the nearest seat to the door. In it sat innocent Thomas Grant whose life was soon to come to an end.

Tattooed Wood lunged at him, his arm and hand making a downward motion, and then sprang back from his victim. One passenger who saw the attack said it was 'quick and forceful, like a boxer' another said Wood had 'an evil look on his face'.

Thomas Grant shouted, 'I've been stabbed', and Wood said in an emotionless voice, 'He's dead.' The entire incident lasted just five seconds.

It was shortly before midday and the train was taking men, women and children home to see their loved ones. It was en route to that most British of West Country seaside resorts, Paignton, on the 'English Riviera', and now it had turned into a high-speed, bloody nightmare.

Quite understandably pandemonium broke out. All the passengers, including the youngsters, fled the carriage. By now the train manager was on the scene and he managed to lock the sliding door with Wood inside the carriage. He was trapped and he knew it. He tried unsuccessfully to break the door down before trying to prise it open with his left hand, kicking it in his frustration and rage as he did so.

The terrified train manager recalled: 'He then realised that he could not get through and I just froze and watched him. He went berserk and he was kicking the door that I had just locked, using his foot to kick backwards. He was then kicking the rubber between the two doors, going absolutely berserk. I could see him going mental. Thank God I had locked that door. He was just like a mad man. I was afraid he was going to kill me.'

A female member of the train staff said: 'I will not forget the look on his face. He looked like a lunatic, a crazed person. I have never been so scared in my life.'

When the train made an emergency stop at Oxenholme station in Cumbria, tattooed Wood escaped through a train window after smashing it with a hammer and throwing a fire extinguisher through the window. The passengers who immediately rushed back into the carriage to Thomas could do nothing. He was already dead from the single stab wound to his chest which went through his lung and an artery. Police were to find the knife, broken in half, nearby.

Desperate to escape, Wood fled across fields and was given a lift by a passing farmer, excusing the blood on himself by claiming he had cut himself on a barbed-wire fence. His freedom was not to last long, and he was arrested at a roadblock as the farmer drove him to a bus station.

As is often the case after such an attack, he then compounded the barbarity of the assault by concocting a 'defence' that was so obviously untrue it almost defied belief. He said he had been 'intimidated' by Thomas on the platform and that he had only intended to threaten him, but was knocked over by the sliding door.

Initial reports of the senseless attack were confused, suggesting, erroneously, that Thomas had gone to the aid of a woman who was involved in an argument with Wood. Perhaps if that had been the case then the stabbing would have made 'sense' – albeit only in the twisted mind of a savage like Wood – but it was not so. In truth it was an attack without rhyme or reason.

If Thomas's tragically brief young life had already been one of achievement, the same could not be said of Wood.

Raised on a tough council estate in Skelmersdale, he was the eldest of five children and he was repeatedly in trouble at school for fighting and vandalism. His chicken-packer father Paul and mother Elizabeth McGuffie did little to control him.

At the age of eight he was diagnosed with behavioural problems and went on to attend a series of special schools in Skelmersdale, Liverpool and Yorkshire. By the time Wood was in his teens, his mother, who had been subjected to regular beatings by his father, returned to her native Huddersfield. Wood's behaviour only got worse as a result, and in 1999, when he was only sixteen, he picked up his first conviction, for theft and shoplifting. He left school without any qualifications, working briefly in a fruit-packing factory and as a car valet before settling into life on the dole.

To kill time he'd hang around with other youths on the estate, smoking dope, drinking and vandalising houses, shops and cars just for fun of it.

Initially adults would reprimand him, but as he grew bigger and stronger that became a dangerous thing to do. In seven years Wood was before the courts for a total of forty offences including thirteen thefts and burglaries, four offences against property, twelve driving offences, eight breaches of bail and one offence of carrying a lock knife, for which he was jailed for twenty-one days in 2003.

He began to use cannabis more frequently – he was probably high during the train attack – and he was acquiring a growing reputation for violence. People steered clear of him. Poor Thomas Grant was unfortunate not to be able to do that.

It wasn't just Thomas's family who were devastated by the news: his teachers and friends echoed their feelings of loss.

Oakham headmaster Dr Joseph Spence said staff and pupils at the school were 'devastated' by his death. 'All who study and work at Oakham School have been deeply saddened to hear of the tragic and violent death of Tom Grant,' he said. 'Tom Grant had many friends and touched the lives of all his teachers and peers. He was a vivid personality and was a role model for younger pupils. Always alert to the needs of others, he will live long in the memories of everyone who knew him.

'I suppose it is somewhat of a cliché to say that the good always die young, but in Tom's case this couldn't be more true. He was a real winner in every aspect of the phrase. Tom was very modest about his achievements. But the truth is that he was the kind of pupil that every teacher wished would take up their subject. Just two weeks before he died he returned to the school for our inspection of the Combined Cadet Force. He seemed so alive and so buoyed with enthusiasm. It is very difficult to come to terms with the fact that his vitality has been taken away in the most brutal and violent way imaginable.'

Charles Jacks, eighteen, who shared a boarding house with Tom for five years, said his friends were 'devastated' by the news. 'He was a genuine guy, there was nothing affected about him. You could call him one of the lads. He was a real joker, and really popular. He was looking to apply to Sandhurst. He'd been to all the talks about it at university. He couldn't wait to go there.'

He said Tom's group of friends had called each other to offer comfort when the news broke. 'I couldn't believe it at first, when I heard the news. Within a few hours of us finding out everyone was ringing around and comforting everyone. We're all devastated.'

Staff at St Andrews were also stunned to hear of his death, describing him as a 'bright, extremely able student'. University Vice-Principal Stephen Magee said: 'We are deeply saddened by this news. There is a palpable sense of shock here. To have lost someone so young in such circumstances is utterly tragic. Our deepest sympathies are with Tom's mother and father.'

A month after his death Thomas's funeral was held at the picturesque sixteenth-century Cille Choirill church, near Roy Bridge in the Scottish Highlands. His parents, Kenny and Pat, decided to bury their son in the area – where Thomas used to love walking – because of his father's family connections in the region. He was buried close to the grave of his great-uncle, Bishop Kenneth Grant, who was a prisoner of war for five years during the Second World War.

The service was conducted by Roy Bridge parish priest Monsignor Thomas Wynne, St Andrews University chaplain the Revd Jamie Walker and RAF chaplain the Revd Peter Mills. Father Wynne said: 'It was a very moving service. There were representatives from different parts of the country who attended and were there to see Thomas laid to rest among his ancestors in the peace and silence of Cille Choirill.'

It was in November 2006 that Wood appeared before Preston Crown Court accused of killing poor Thomas. He had, thankfully, decided to plead guilty to murder, and the ordeal of reliving in detail the events of that train journey would not have to be replayed and recounted as they would have been in a trial.

Prosecutor Tim Holroyde, QC, described the horrific stabbing as a 'cold-blooded' attack on 'a young man who was simply minding his own business'.

He added: 'Far from being provocative, he had merely responded minimally to what anyone would regard as an unusual remark.'

The judge, Mr Justice Openshaw, said the teenager 'was no doubt concerned to hear such a threat made, but he did nothing more, just a look. It cost him his life.'

In jailing shaven-headed Wood, now twenty-two, for life, he noted that he had decided to plead guilty only six weeks before his scheduled trial. There was a recommendation that he serve at least twenty-one years, later reduced to twenty on appeal.

Telling the killer that his sentence had to reflect the public's outrage and revulsion, as well as the 'indescribable loss' suffered by Tom's family and friends he said, 'It is surely relevant that a life so full of achievement and promise has ended in such a cruel and wicked manner. This is a truly shocking case.'

Wood, dressed in a dark blue tracksuit, had stared at the oak panelling in front of him throughout the hearing. As the life sentence was passed, he rose from his seat and was led away, his face devoid of emotion.

After the case, one of the key figures in that day, nineteen-year-old Sarah Chadwick was interviewed and gave her version of what had happened – and her reaction to her ex-boyfriend's frenzy.

'Tom didn't deserve to die and I am so sorry for his family and friends. I wished it was me that Thomas had killed,' she said.

She recalled that Wood was hurling abuse at her on the station in Carlisle after she told him their relationship was over when Thomas Grant looked at them. 'Thomas said to him, "What the f*** are you looking at? I'm going to stab you in a minute." I had no idea he was carrying a kitchen knife. I thought it was best for me to keep out of his way so I sat with my auntie and my cousins when we got on the train. He was still furious and kept walking up and down the carriage. I'll never forget what his face looked like. It was contorted, all screwed up, and he looked so angry. He looked like pure evil. I was terrified.'

Sarah then heard the cry 'I've been stabbed.'

She said: 'I knew instinctively that Thomas had stabbed the boy from the platform. Everyone just sat there, frozen. Then I realised I would be next. I ran after my family to the first-class carriage. The door wouldn't open and I was banging on it, I was so scared. It finally opened and other people from our carriage came in. The train guard managed to get everyone to safety and Thomas was locked in the original carriage on his own.

'The train stopped but he was trying to get to me, banging on the door. Then he smashed the window and got out of the carriage and was running alongside the one I was in, looking for me. He wanted to kill me. I was so scared. I will never forget the look on his face. It was twisted with anger. It was pure evil. He'd already killed that poor boy and I knew I was next. My auntie told me to duck and I just cowered under a table for what seemed like an eternity until the police arrived.'

She had first met Wood when he was released from a prison sentence. She allowed him to move in with her and soon discovered he was prone to violent outbursts of temper, but nevertheless took him to stay with her aunt in Cumbria. Wood made several threats to kill her during that week, attacked her in front of her young cousins and tried to throw her out of a window. It was then that, on several occasions, he punched her in the stomach even though he knew that she thought she might be pregnant.

On that fateful May morning en route to the station,

Sarah told him they were finished, and
on the platform there was the row about

'I wish I'd never met Thomas and I am so
what he did to that boy. At first I blamed myself
thought if I hadn't been with Thomas then he wouldn't
have been on the train that day and his victim would
still be alive. The sadness will never leave me. I'm just
so sorry and I wish I could turn back time.'

Detective Superintendent Michael Field, who led the
investigation, had his own views on the tragedy: 'This
sentence should be reflected upon by anyone who gets
involved in knife crime. If people want to carry knives,
they will be subject to search and arrest in certain
circumstances. Such crime will not be tolerated on the
railway or anywhere else in society. Tom Grant was a
young man with everything to live for and an extremely
bright future ahead of him. Tragically, he was the victim
of a random attack that he could not have done
anything to prevent. He did not provoke Thomas Wood,
he was simply in the wrong place at the wrong time.'

As is almost inevitably the case, the saddest words
come from those who are left to mourn. In Thomas
Grant's case it was his parents who tried to put into
words that which is indescribable.

Speaking after his death, his parents said: 'As a family,
we are deeply shocked and immeasurably saddened by
the untimely death of our beloved only son, Thomas
Peter Grant. Thomas had achieved much during his

ineteen years. He was happily studying medieval history and Arabic at St Andrews University, having left Oakham School, Rutland, in the summer of 2005. He was a keen hillwalker, notably in the West Highlands and also participated in a number of sports, including football, water polo, swimming and rugby. As a keen Liverpool fan he was overjoyed at the recent FA Cup Final victory. One of his treasured possessions was his iPod, which was never far from his person and contained a wide mixture of rock music. Travel was high on his agenda and included sailing in Norfolk with his Oakham pals, hillwalking and skiing in the Austrian Alps and a special visit to Oman last year. He had so much to live for. He was a wonderful gift to us, his parents. He has left us with vibrant memories and examples of how to give the most to life and other people, and we sincerely hope that all those with whom he came into contact were enriched, in however small capacity, by his personality.'

Later, after the verdict, Mr Grant said: 'We would like to record our gratitude for the support and guidance of the British Transport Police since May 27. We also wish to thank the train crew for all they did in trying to help Thomas after he was attacked and for their bravery in the face of the ensuing horror. The circumstances of Thomas's death have now been clarified. Thomas did not act as a Good Samaritan intervening in an argument on the train, as the media suggested in the days following his death. Instead, he was attacked as he sat next to his luggage, minding his own business.

'This is what makes his death all the more shocking and unforgivable. He had great potential to make a significant contribution to society, but this potential has been needlessly wasted. For us, the way ahead is dark, lit only by memories of our dear son, by the love and support of family and friends and by the spirit of Thomas's wonderful young friends and colleagues from school and university.

'My wife and I now ask the media to refrain from approaching us, any of Thomas's family and friends and, indeed, any of the organisations with which he was involved.

'Finally, it is our hope that everyone who knew Thomas will be sustained by the positive and generous approach to other people which he showed in his all too short life.'

6

It is a vision from Hell. A gang of young people, including girls, racing down a street in one of the greatest cities in the world, screaming 'Kill him, kill him.' Their target, a boy of just sixteen. And that's exactly what they did, they killed Kodjo Yenga. Some of the twelve-strong group, armed with knives, bats and a bull-terrier dog, were even laughing as the life was ebbing out of him.

Kodjo – his name meant 'Born on a Monday' – had been born in the Congo, formerly Zaïre, one of the most violent countries in the world, a name synonymous with brutality. His mother had brought him to Britain to be safe, to be away from the barbarity and violence that was endemic in the central African country. He was a bright, academic boy who hoped to go to university.

Yet here he was in the teeming, comfortable streets of Hammersmith Grove in London, being stabbed to death. How had it happened? How had a group of boys, some still in school uniform, turned into such savages?

The answer, at least in this case, lay in the gang culture that bonded his attackers into an uncaring, violent mob. Their tactic was to challenge non-members to a one-on-one fight and then ambush them. That was how Kodjo came to die in the arms of his girlfriend on 14 March 2007.

It was a Wednesday afternoon. Kodjo and his girlfriend of two years, Cookie, had just been asked by a security guard to leave the large Hammersmith shopping centre as they had a puppy with them and it wouldn't stop barking.

They met a group of five teenage boys, some still in school uniform as it was only 4.30 p.m. One of them Tirrell Davis, fifteen, said to Kodjo, 'I hear you want to fight me.' Kodjo refused, saying, 'I don't want to fight with you because you're a little boy.'

Eventually he had to agree to the challenge and the group, now about ten-strong but occasionally splitting up, left the large Hammersmith Broadway roundabout behind them. Both Davis and Kodjo made calls on their mobiles and a backpack was passed between Davis and another boy, Brandon Richmond.

Kodjo was aware that only a week earlier a friend of his had accepted a similar challenge from the gang now assembled, only to be set upon and beaten up badly by them. They even poured boiling water on his face and arms.

Kodjo's girlfriend recalled later: 'I remember the day so clearly . . . it was two days before my second anniversary with Kodjo. He had been getting texts from someone challenging him to a one-on-one fight, but didn't want to get involved. Then we saw the boy, waving a knife in the street. I tried to stay calm but there were loads of them and they were all egging on the one with the knife.

'Some of them were chanting "Kill him, kill him" – it was horrible. The gang was laughing and some of them had bats.'

'You could see in their faces that they didn't care who they hurt. They thought it was funny. I saw the knife and I knew that either one of us or both of us would die. Kizzle [her pet name for Kodjo] told me to run for my life, but I couldn't leave him. I tried to fight the boy off, but I was being held back by another one. I shouted "Run, run!" but they were hunting him down and he couldn't get away. When he dropped to the floor I knew they'd stabbed him. That's when I ran over to him. I held him and he was still breathing and saying it would be all right as I was begging him not to die.

'The gang just laughed and ran off. An ambulance came and they told me to get away because the shock of me screaming might hurt him. By the time he got to hospital he was gone.'

'Kodjo was wearing a white T-shirt when he was stabbed and it just turned red. I kept screaming "Don't die. Don't die. Don't leave me here!" But he said, "I love you. Don't worry. I'll be OK."'

She added: 'He was the one who gave me the nickname Cookie because he said I was sweet. We had been going out for about seven months when he told me he loved me.

'He was fun, but really serious about getting a good education and that has really encouraged me to try harder at school. He was so talented, writing songs with his group Ride 4 Life.'

The young girl, who never wanted her full name known, added, 'I was fourteen and I watched my boyfriend die. A lot of people say, "You're impressive, you look like nothing's happened to you." But I'm really trying to get the message across that it's painful. I lost my boyfriend, but, even worse, I knew who they [the killers] were. So it was a double barrel of hurt. You're looking at consequences. You're looking at crying mothers, and funerals and you're also looking at me. I'm not saying I'm that important, but the girlfriends do go through so much.'

Tragic as his death was, the slaying of Kodjo was not an isolated incident. Around the time of his death one military surplus store in London reported a 'roaring trade' in stab-proof waistcoats at £120 a time that once were bought by nightclub bouncers or the armed forces. Now it was worried parents buying them for their children. The youngsters were so small the waistcoats hardly fitted under their blazers.

One newspaper obtained figures from the majority of the police forces in the country showing that in a three-month period that year there had been 5,500 serious crimes involving knives. It worked out at one every twenty-four minutes and included fifty-five knife-related murders, more than 2,000 stabbings and almost 2,500 muggings at knifepoint. During just April, May and June, the Metropolitan Police in London recorded 1,580 offences – more than a quarter of the national total. Seventeen people were stabbed or robbed at knifepoint in the capital every day.

Lyn Costello, for Mothers Against Murder and Aggression, declared that the figures were no surprise to her because she had always said the published ones were too conservative.

She said: 'It just shows that we have to do something now. We have to go into schools to talk to children about carrying knives and explain to them what it does to families and the people around those who get injured and killed. If they are educated and they still break the law, then they should be given tougher sentences.

'We are losing control of our streets. People are frightened to go out at night, frightened to go to the shop at night. We are talking to people daily who are scared of living in this country.'

By that summer there were an estimated 170 gangs

on the streets of London, some of them with as many as a hundred members. Other gangs operated in major cities elsewhere, meaning that on any night there were thousands of young men on the streets of Britain who were ready to use force to achieve whatever they wanted, no matter at what cost.

Detective Chief Superintendent Barry Norman told the *Sunday Telegraph*, 'Serious youth violence is the biggest problem we have today in London – with the possible exception of terrorism. Nothing frightens people more, and when that violence takes place in a group setting, it is all the more shocking. If I could achieve just one more thing in my service, it would be to wake up the whole of London to this problem. Trying to suppress gang crime on a day-to-day basis is like holding a football underwater. Eventually it just comes flying back in your face.'

A year-long government study had concluded that black teenagers urgently needed role models to divert them from the world of gangs and criminality.

Mr Norman said: 'How difficult must it be for a parent to bring up a kid in some of these areas? How difficult must it be to be a kid and to make the right choice when sometimes the easiest way to be "safe" is to belong to a group of other kids? It's an awful situation and there is no short-term solution. The only way to stop today's children becoming tomorrow's problem is to invest in them when they are young. The best thing that can happen from the tragedy of this year – with eighteen teenagers murdered in London – is that we get new money, new investments, new partnerships and we invest in the long term.

'This mustn't be seen as just a police issue. The health service, the education service, social services and the Home Office all need to do a whole lot more. I sense there is a real appetite for this, but we have got to grasp the opportunity and work together.'

Norman Brennan, a police officer and director of the Victims of Crime Trust, said a child was stabbed to death in Britain every two weeks, and knife killings outnumbered gun homicides three to one: 'Knife crime is out of control and kids carry them like fashion accessories.'

Newspapers were regularly publishing details of the latest attacks and carrying stomach-churning 'tables' of the latest victims as they totted up the 'score'. One child suspended from school for brandishing a blade was just five. Truly, a world gone crazy.

And that madness was touched on at Kodjo's funeral in May when his uncle Lubi Takson made a heartfelt plea following a moving requiem mass attended by hundreds of mourners.

Mr Takson said after the service, held at St Francis of Assisi Church in Notting Hill: 'Thank God we are at last taking our beloved Kodjo to his final place of rest, where he will surely enjoy eternal and divine peace.

There's no need to remind everyone how painful it is to lose a child at this tender age. However, if there are lessons to be learned, the authorities ought to do more in terms of providing support to the bereaved families, and parents should be encouraging the youngsters to cooperate with the police in giving evidence whenever they witness an incident. Not only will this attitude make the police job much easier during investigations, but the society in which we all live could become a better place.'

He added that the family would be campaigning to make sure no other person would have to bury a loved one under the same circumstances.

Father Shaun Middleton, who led the service, called on the many youngsters in the congregation to help change the world they were growing up in: 'There are many young people here today and you are the future. You have the capacity to shape and build a new society.' He added: 'Many of you know how difficult it can be to live in a city like ours. A city where old people are fearful, a city where parents are afraid to let their children play in the street for fear something will happen to them or where a human life is extinguished without thought or feeling. I appeal to young people here today to use the tragedy of this event and in your hearts to reject the culture of violence and hostility which pervades our streets.'

He finished his address by saying: 'I challenge you

to become ambassadors for peace. This is the most fitting tribute you can pay to Kodjo.'

Many of the congregation were dressed in white or wore white scarves in honour of the murdered teenager, and a large portrait of Kodjo was placed at the front of the church next to his coffin.

So who were the savages who ended the life of Kodjo, an academically bright boy whose mother insisted he be home at nine o'clock at night? They were members of a gang called the MDP, standing either for Murder Dem Pussies or Money, Drugs, Power. Whichever meaning they attached to their initials spelt trouble as far as law-abiding people were concerned. One of the ways of becoming a member of MDP was to stab someone. Their favourite 'pets' were Staffordshire bull terriers, handy for intimidating victims.

Kodjo's death had been enacted in front of scores of people and, with the aid of CCTV footage which had captured the start of the ordeal at the shopping centre, arrests soon followed.

So it was that a detailed account of that afternoon was told to an Old Bailey jury early the next year, when six young men, aged fourteen to seventeen, stood trial for his murder. Sir Allan Green, QC, prosecuting, described the scene that day:

A woman, Deepika Kohli, was walking up Hammersmith Grove with her child in a pushchair when she spotted Kodjo running away. 'Behind him was a group of ten black youths. She noticed two girls as well. She could hear a few members of the group shouting 'catch him, kill him'. Two or three members of the group caught him and appeared to stab the back of his jacket, before Kodjo managed to slip their grasp and get away. The group seemed 'happy, they were laughing and smiling' and they ran off.

Kodjo had agreed to have a one-to-one fight after a member of the MDP gang challenged him to a fight, the jury was told. He agreed despite Cookie urging him not to get involved. When the pair confronted each other on a Hammersmith side street, another eight or nine boys, including one with a bull terrier, arrived to back up their gangmate, and one of them appeared to have a Stanley knife behind his back.

Kodjo said to him: 'Do you think you are a big boy because you have a knife to me?' Only to be told in reply, 'I don't care. I want you to respect me.'

It was as the others appeared that Kodjo realised it was an ambush.

Cookie kicked one of the attackers who fell to the ground but he got up and threatened to 'shank, or stab her'. Sir Allan continued: 'Another boy grabbed her from behind, we say to stop her from intervening in the attack on Kodjo.'

Kodjo ran away as she shouted at him, encouraging him to escape, but as he tried to escape he stumbled over a motorbike and the gang's bull terrier.

Passers-by, including a policeman, who was driving past, stopped to try and help Kodjo who lay dying in his girlfriend's arms.

His eyes were half open, but blood was soaking through his shirt, and he died later in hospital.

A trademark of the MDP is to attack boys who are not part of the gang by suggesting a one-to-one fight outside their local area, according to Sir Allan, culminating in a 'serious assault with various weapons'.

Another witness was teacher Angela Quinn who was cycling down Hammersmith Grove when she saw a group of youths running ahead of her, some in the road and some on the pavement. They were shouting and very excited, the court heard.

Sir Allan said: 'She heard a girl shout "he's going to stab him", then the same girl shouted: "He stabbed him."'

After going into a nearby shop to ask someone to call for help, Ms Quinn began pushing her bicycle down the road and came face-to-face with a youngster about six feet in front of her holding a knife.

Sir Allan told the jury: 'The boy had a knife in his hand. The knife was shiny, shaped about five inches long and less than an inch wide. She had got the impression the handle was black. There was wet blood on the blade of the knife. The boy was holding it out at arm's length with the blade pointing upwards. He looked proud as if he had done something by way of an accomplishment.'

Ms Quinn asked him: 'What have you done?'

The boy told her: 'Shut your mouth.' Ms Quinn then called him 'a bastard'.

Although they all denied the charge of murder, five of the gang who surrounded Kodjo that Wednesday afternoon were found guilty of killing him.

Brandon Richmond, fourteen, who was just thirteen when the attack took place, and Tirrel Davis, aged seventeen by the time of the court case, were convicted of murder and sentenced to minimum detention of fifteen years – the juvenile equivalent of a life sentence.

Kurtis Yemoh, seventeen, Michel Williams, fifteen, and Jamel Bridgeman, fifteen, were found guilty of manslaughter and each sentenced to ten years' detention to be followed by a period of five years on licence. Yemoh had been in court earlier on the day that Kodjo died, on charges of theft of a bicycle and intimidating a witness, but was granted bail, although police objected. A sixth accused was acquitted.

Sentencing the five, Judge Christopher Moss said: 'You are part of a gang culture that casts a dreadful influence over the youth of our cities and which led almost inevitably to the tragedy seen so vividly here. I can't pretend to know the solution to what has become a serious social problem – that is for others to address in our schools, families and the government – but the courts must send out a clear message that the violent taking of life by youngsters will be severely punished.'

The judge added that it was an example of the 'needless loss of another young life' because of knives. He said: 'All of you come from decent and caring backgrounds which makes the situation all the more worrying.'

He said the sentences had to be a deterrent in the face of what had become a serious social problem.

Detective Superintendent Matthew Horne called on parents to make sure they knew where their children were at night and what they were up to. He said: 'Some of the boys were only thirteen when they committed these crimes – children, only just teenagers. To their parents I would ask this: What were your kids doing? Where did you think they were at the times these boys were so brutally killed?

'That's a message to all of us who are parents – we have to take some responsibility to ensure our children are brought up as honest and decent human beings.'

Another senior policeman, Detective Superintendent Vic Rae, said: 'Kodjo was a bright student, his whole life was before him when it was taken away from him in a moment. Young men reading of this crime must consider the effects of a moment's bravado on the lives of foes, friends and all families. That three of the defendants were only thirteen at the time of the murder, little more than children, is shocking to all concerned.'

As is so often the case, the pain of a grieving mother is almost too overwhelming to bear even thinking about. In her impact statement read out when her son's killers were convicted Ladjua Lesele said: 'I stand before you as a broken mother whose prayers, dreams and hopes for the bright future of her beloved son were cruelly and needlessly crushed when he was brutally murdered in Hammersmith Grove.

'These cold-blooded children tormented and stabbed my wonderful and innocent son, while they screamed, "Kill him, kill him." I only have one thing to say to those who murdered Kodjo. As you spilled and touched his blood, no matter how many times you wash your hands, his blood will stay on them.'

Speaking on the steps of the Old Bailey she added: 'I would call upon all young people to stop using weapons, to avoid being in a gang and to stop all violent acts. I implore you all to focus on your education, contribute positively to your community and most importantly to do the things that will make your family and parents proud of you. I want lessons to be learned from Kodjo's brutal murder.'

Earlier she had said, 'Kodjo was very friendly, he was very popular. My son was never a part of a gang and his name was never in the list of any gang. He was a good Christian. We never kept secrets from each other. My life with my boy was fantastic. We loved each other. We were really inseparable. I will miss him all my life.'

Describing her son as an 'exemplary child' and 'gifted scholar', she added: 'Since [Kodjo's death] my life has changed profoundly and I find it increasingly difficult to battle through the overwhelming pain and loss I feel. Only other parents who have lost a beloved child in similar circumstances to mine can understand and feel the pain I am going through. I feel very let down by the bureaucratic administration system in the town hall and the limited support I received during this extremely difficult time.'

Making a plea for an end to the gang violence that saw twenty-seven murders of children and teenagers in London the previous year, and eleven up to April in 2008, she said: 'I ask every young person with a knife or gun to stop what you are doing and think about the ripples of pain you leave eternally with the family whose loved one you thoughtlessly killed in a moment of madness that will also change your life for ever. No matter what the outcome of the trial or the future, my son Kodjo will never come home again, and that breaks my heart.'

Ironically, keen musician Kodjo had been interviewed by MTV some months before his death about the problem of knife crime. 'Stabbings are getting worse but the media is also making it bigger than what it is,' he said. And when asked about the prevalence of knife crime he replied, 'I don't think it happens all the time but it happens quite a lot. Most young men and girls I know carry knives around for protection to threaten others. I don't think it's a good idea to carry knives around. I wouldn't, because I'm not in that type of situation.'

7

Knife crime is horrific. When one man decides to plunge sharpened metal into the body of another man, the consequences are devastating. Permanent injury or handicap, scarring, a loss of faculties, even death, they all follow as surely as night follows day.

But even that vision can become more grotesque, an even greater mirror of the malaise running through our society, when the two people involved are not men but young, very young, women. Truly a world on the edge of an abyss.

One, a girl just weeks past her fifteenth birthday yet high on drink and drugs. The other, an eighteen-year-old mother of ten weeks on her first night out since giving birth. That was the confrontation that took place shortly before midnight on 2 August 2007 in an alley in the north-east of England between Jordan Jobson and Samantha Madgin.

Samantha, who had dreams of becoming a model,

had a baby son Callum earlier in the summer and was already talking about going on holiday with the rest of her family and the tiny child to the Dominican Republic. The week before her life ended in such a bloody fashion she had moved into a flat of her own after saving up by working full-time for her pub-landlord father.

As she had not had a babysitter for an evening until that fatal night, this was the first time she had been out since becoming a mother. She spent a large part of what was to be her last night alive talking about her baby, and even went back to make sure Callum was all right at about 10.30 p.m. before deciding to go out again.

Jordan Jobson's night had been different. The fifteen-year-old schoolgirl had already drunk six cans of lager and three-quarters of a bottle of vodka washed down with cola, as well as taking seven or eight lines of cocaine. She was with two male friends at a flat in Wallsend – the area of Newcastle once renowned for ship-building, but also famous for being the birthplace of milkman's son Gordon Sumner, alias pop millionaire Sting – as the effects of her night began to take their toll.

The two men with her left to telephone for some more drugs, only to return soon afterwards telling her 'there was bother and they were going to sort it out,' and then she heard shouting outside.

Jobson took an eight-inch knife from the kitchen – a decision that was to result shortly in Samantha's young life ending in such a sad manner – and went outside. Her reasoning: 'Because I wanted to frighten them away and sort out the trouble and to protect myself.'

Jobson's two friends were arguing with two of Samantha's and then she noticed the doomed young mother who was holding a bottle. Samantha, she was later to claim, was holding it at shoulder height and said to her, using local dialect to make a disparaging remark: 'Are you with these rajies?'

Jobson said she had been holding the knife with the blade up her arm because she had not wanted to use it and so it could not be seen, but when Samantha got closer, she had moved the knife out so the young mother could see it.

'We got closer together. I thought she was going to hit me with the bottle. I showed her the knife in the hope she would move away.' But poor Samantha didn't and the two teenage girls started to fight. Jobson said she began to wave her hands around 'to get her off me' and her version of events was that she was not conscious of the fact she had the knife in her hand and that all those movements were resulting in Samantha being stabbed time and again. In total she suffered one wound to the face, four to the left arm, two to the right arm and three to the chest. One wound went through her right hand, another blow cut off a finger as she tried to protect herself. She fell against a white garage door, staining it with her blood, and took some steps in the direction of her home before falling over. She probably died in less than a minute. The fatal blow had gone through the left side of her chest.

'When I tried to get her away from me, my hands pushed out. I can't remember when that was. It wasn't right at the beginning and it wasn't at the very end either,' Jobson maintained, saying she never intended to kill or cause Samantha serious harm and her intention during the fight was 'just to get her off me'.

That was how she saw the events of that night.

It would be comforting to think this was an isolated example of the havoc a knife brings, but it wasn't. In fact it was just another example of knife crime in the area.

Train operators Nexus and the local Newcastle City Council even included anti-knife messages in a legal graffiti campaign they launched with the messages 'Turn In Your Knife Before It's Turned On You', and 'Don't Carry Knives For Thrills Cos They Kill', sprayed on murals at a rail station.

Sadly it wasn't just Samantha's death that inspired the campaign.

Mark Smith, a sixteen-year-old, was stabbed in the neck with a kitchen knife during a drink-fuelled row in Newcastle's West End and a teenager was jailed for eighteen months for his manslaughter.

The same month, fifteen-year-old Shane Jackson was stabbed fifty-five times with a kitchen knife by his best friend Billy Dunwoody after a drinking binge. Dunwoody, who was subsequently jailed for life for murder, was so drunk he was seen 'shaking with laughter' after the killing. He later told police he could not remember the attack, adding: 'I wish I could turn the clock back. If I had not had a drink it would not have happened.'

Christopher Johnston, nineteen, was stabbed repeatedly with a samurai sword as he drank with friends on a playing-field near his Tyneside home. His windpipe was severed and his chest sliced through by his attacker David Barton, twenty, who was locked up for life.

And, as we have already seen, in one case that had horrified the nation, new father Kevin Johnson, twenty-two, of Sunderland, was stabbed in the heart after he asked a gang of rowdy youths outside his home to be quiet. Three local teenagers were convicted of stabbing Kevin to death and given life terms. There were many other cases too.

Home Office figures were to show that between April 2007 and April 2008 there were 351 knife crimes in the Northumbria Police area, while in Durham ninety-three people became the victims of knife-carriers during the same period. The figures referred to serious violent offences involving blades, ranging from wounding to murder.

Of course, this geographically small part of the country was not suffering an outbreak of knife violence any greater than the rest of the United Kingdom, it was merely reflected the virus that was spreading throughout society.

Figures were also on the increase for young women committing crimes; the number of young women being dealt with by Newcastle courts rose from 472 in 2003–4 to 541 in 2006–7.

In a ritual that was becoming depressingly familiar throughout Britain, hundreds gathered to pay their tribute to a young life needlessly lost.

More than 700 mourners were at St Bernadette's RC church, Wallsend, when Samantha was laid to rest. Her father Stan cradled her baby son, accompanied by her mother Alison and sister Carly, sixteen, while they entered the church where Samantha had celebrated her first holy communion. Among those carrying the pink coffin into the church to the sound of 'Big Big World' by Emilia, one of her favourite songs, were Callum's father Stephen McKenzie, twenty-six, and Samantha's brother Lee.

Father Anthony Donaghue read out a tribute to the popular teenager, which was relayed into the churchyard over a loudspeaker for the hundreds who could not get into the crowded church. He said: 'When she was pregnant she used to wonder what the baby would be like, she used to wonder what kind of person the baby would become when he was older. Mother and child shared each other's lives for sixty-eight life-giving days, so very brief, but so very special.'

The Eva Cassidy version of 'Somewhere Over The Rainbow' – Samantha loved *The Wizard of Oz* – echoed out of the church. Her younger sister also gave a reading from the first letter of St Paul to the Thessalonians and her aunt said a prayer.

Father Donaghue added: 'I know that you, Alison and Stan, and all your family and friends are determined to let Callum know what a beautiful and compassionate person his mother was. Life was fulfilling and really worthwhile for Samantha over the last few months. She was always willing to uplift those who were down, she was outgoing, understanding, caring, friendly, very energetic and a good listener. She brought us joy, she enriched our lives, she had a heart full of love and compassion, we will always cherish her.'

Afterwards more than 300 mourners attended the internment at Holy Cross Cemetery, Wallsend. The family were swamped with grief at this time. In a terrible twist of fate Samantha's uncle Gary Madgin had died in a car crash eleven days after her murder, just hours after hearing that his uncle, Bob Higginson, had died in Canada during a wedding.

In February the next year Jobson's trial began at Newcastle Crown Court. She had already admitted manslaughter but denied murder. Alistair MacDonald, prosecuting, told the jury the fifteen-year-old had been drinking and taking cocaine before the attack, which happened after an argument between Samantha's friends and two men. He said that Samantha was trying to stop the argument and was heard to shout 'come away'. 'It is the prosecution's case that this was a sustained and determined attack by the person who wielded the knife. That is supported by the evidence given by the expert forensic scientists. She struggled with her attacker as she moved down the road to the place where her body lay.'

Mr MacDonald added: 'The sole issue for you to decide is whether she committed murder or manslaughter. Anybody who has a weapon of that sort with them in a public place, who inflicts that number of injuries on a person, intends to cause, at the very least, really serious harm.' He added that Samantha was unarmed: 'Samantha Madgin had no chance whatsoever within the course of this struggle.'

He told the jury that some of Samantha's injuries were defensive and although an ambulance arrived soon after the attack, the paramedics could do nothing to save her. Mr MacDonald said that the defendant was not present at the initial fracas, which occurred at around 11.30 p.m.

Although Jobson had not been present when the row began, 'It is clear, we submit, that she came out and started into the back alley and within a few seconds Samantha Madgin was stabbed. Why did she have a knife in her hand? Did she take it out to deliberately seek confrontation with Samantha Madgin?'

He said a witness overheard a conversation between a female, believed to be the defendant, and a man soon afterwards.

'He could hear the man say "Did you stab her?" and the female voice replied "yes".'

Jobson handed herself over to the police and they found her discarded knife down a drain the next day. She was found guilty of the murder and told she must serve at least fifteen years behind bars. Sentencing her, Judge David Hodson said her victim was unarmed when she was repeatedly stabbed with the large kitchen knife.

'This is yet another tragic example of the all-too-familiar pattern of young people taking excessive quantities of alcohol, of mixing drink and dangerous drugs and resorting to the use of knives at will, he said. 'That combustible combination we see happening all too frequently, and the tragic and fatal consequences we have seen again.' He added: 'One can hardly imagine the devastation and emptiness the Madgin family now feel.'

Samantha's mother Alison bravely tried to put those indescribable feelings into words: 'Every day has been a struggle and I imagine that is what the rest of our lives will feel like. Samantha had a zest for life, loved her family, was always loyal to her friends, but the most love was for her son Callum, born on May 25 2007. Samantha and Callum spent sixty-eight days together. All because of the evil that was on the streets that fatal night, Samantha will never enjoy any of those special moments a mother is privileged to have. As a mother myself, I long to hear Samantha's voice, smell her, kiss her, feel her, hug her hard.'

She said: 'It is just total devastation. Little things like a happy moment are tinged with sadness. We miss her so much. It has ruined all our lives for ever. The pain gets worse each day. Samantha's sister Carly is having counselling and her grandparents have taken it really bad. The house is not the same without her. It's so quiet. I miss her friends coming around and her laughing. I'm worrying about going back to work and I can't face Christmas. But it was Samantha's favourite day and the only time she'd get up early, so we're going to have a family dinner for her and spoil Callum.'

Alison, forty-two, of Wallsend, was bringing up Callum – by then six months old – and revealed she was dreading the moment when he found out what happened to his mum.

'The only benefit with Callum being a baby is he does not know anything yet, but unfortunately there will be a moment in his life when it is going to affect him and he may need counselling.'

She was later to say: 'I was left wondering who was actually the victim. I sat in court day after day watching the girl who took my daughter's life, and I was amazed at the way the system treated her. She was dressed in fresh clothes every morning, she had her hair nicely done, she had a social worker sitting beside her all the time stroking her hand, all at the taxpayers' expense.

'The lawyers took off their wigs so she wouldn't feel intimidated and every so often she was asked if she was OK because if she was too stressed then the court would take a break. Meanwhile, I listened to the details of how she killed Samantha in an alleyway.

'No one asked me how I was feeling. The state wasn't there to hold my hand. I was just told that if the evidence got too much and I felt myself breaking down, then I should step outside rather than start crying in court.

'It seemed to me that all the sympathy was heaped on the one who did the killing. I watched Jobson all the time for any sign of remorse, but there wasn't a flicker. She never once said she was sorry. She did say she wished she could turn back the clock, but it was clear she meant for her own sake, not for Samantha's.

'Until we change our attitude – and make kids like Jobson think about the consequences before they commit terrible crimes – then we'll carry on losing the battle.'

She added: 'Callum is the treasure that she has left for us.'

Alison recalled how when her daughter was pregnant, she had a frightening dream that almost foretold the future.

'I could see groups of people fighting and screaming and covered in blood, sometimes with their heads cut off. I thought it might be some kind of premonition that Sam was going to have a difficult time in childbirth. Now ... well, it can only have been a warning about the fate that was in the future for her.

'I can't feel hatred at the moment because I have to concentrate my emotions on Callum, but I know she'll still be a young woman when she's free to resume her life.

'Sam wasn't the first victim and won't be the last by a long way unless we do what we know has to be done to tackle the Jobsons of this world.'

She also pointed out: 'In this day and age, it seems that our society is plagued by serious teenage crime and until politicians untie the hands of the police and the courts, this situation can only get worse.

'Ourselves and other families are being forced to endure this heartache on a daily basis, and we beg those in power to put as much thought into the care of victims' families as they do into the welfare of the murderers, who have access to almost unlimited medical, social and legal assistance.'

Samantha's father Stan, a pub landlord, had to cope with the loss too. 'It's just unbelievable what's happened. Samantha would have been a brilliant mam. She absolutely doted on Callum. When I just think of what the bairn's going to miss out on it's just awful. She was absolutely beautiful, she was really bubbly and a right Mickey-taker. I just feel numb, I can't believe she's gone.

'Everything was just so perfect for our whole family before this happened. Samantha was just moving on to a new stage in her life. Having the baby made her grow up that bit more. I built this business up from nothing and things were going so well.

'All her friends have told me that she was talking about Callum all that night, and that she was having a brilliant time. She came into the pub before she went out and she just looked so beautiful. She was just so full of life.

'I just can't get it out of my head what happened to her that night. Everything reminds me of her. Even when I look at my hands I just think of her hand in mine. I just feel numb, from my stomach to my forearms. It would be easy to take if I thought there was a reason for it, but there wasn't.'

He was to add later: 'This should never have been a trial in the first place. She should have held up her hands to what she had done on day one instead of putting my family and my children through this. I'm angry she will go into youth custody and probably come out with ten A levels while Sam is in her grave. But that is British justice these days, it's all about rehabilitation not punishment. Personally I would have dropped her off a cliff.'

'This killer should never be allowed to walk the streets again as we truly believe she is a danger to society. However, the likelihood is that she will be released after serving only a few years and she will still be young enough to lead a long and full life, unlike Samantha. As a family, we will also face the prospect of seeing Samantha's killer after her inevitable release, as she enjoys her freedom and goes about her daily life.'

Detective Chief Inspector Mick Paterson said: 'This was an unnecessary and unprovoked incident where Samantha was tragically killed.

'This is an example of the all-too-frequent incidents where drink and drugs combine together with knives, making for a lethal combination. No amount of custodial sentence will bring Samantha back. Our thoughts are with Samantha's family, particularly her son.'

And Northumbria Police's Deputy Chief Constable David Warcup stressed there was no excuse for carrying a knife, and the courts should treat defendants almost as seriously as those who use one. 'What we have been calling for are measures which will deter people from carrying knives, such as effective sentencing which fully recognises the potential risk associated with carrying a knife, or indeed any other type of offensive weapon.

KNIFE CRIME

Deterrent sentences must not only be applied to those convicted of using a knife to cause injury but should also be applied to those who carry a weapon.'

'Although we have had some success in tackling the problem, there are still far too many incidents involving knives,' he said. 'Northumbria Police will continue to use information and intelligence from the public to tackle the problem, and we will continue to target areas where we believe people are carrying knives and use our powers of stop and search to identify those offenders who still persist.

'We would appeal to anybody who feels that it is brave or tough to carry a knife to think twice. There is simply no excuse for carrying knives in public. Self-defence is not an excuse. Carrying knives in public means that they are only one step away from committing a serious violent crime or indeed they are at risk of having the knife turned on themselves.

'As part of our response to the problem we standardised the force's approach to dealing with offenders carrying knives and have a very clear message for those who are tempted to carry knives or other bladed weapons that anyone found with a knife or pointed weapon after being stopped and searched will be arrested and charged.'

There was to be another painful blow for the dead girl's family when the Court of Appeal in London cut Jobson's minimum sentence from fifteen years to twelve.

Mr Justice David Clarke, sitting with Lord Justice Dyson and Mr Justice Henriques, said the trial judge had not given Jobson enough credit for her young age when she was sentenced. Mr Justice Clarke said the usual starting-point for a murder committed by someone under the age of eighteen after a guilty plea was twelve years. He said: 'The most powerful argument in her favour is her very young age at the time of the offence. The judge drew attention to the drugs and alcohol she had been consuming, but it's clear she was very much put into these activities by her boyfriend.'

He added that Jobson would not necessarily be freed from prison once the twelve years had been completed, but that did nothing to placate Samantha's mother.

'It's like another knife in the heart for our family,' Alison said. 'I'm just gutted. Devastated. It doesn't matter how many years she gets, it's not going to bring Samantha back, but it should be a life for a life.

'How would these judges feel if it was their daughter who was murdered? They'll probably never know. The pain is indescribable.

'She's still never shown any remorse. To me she is a natural born killer. It was in her, it didn't matter what age she was. This doesn't say much for the justice system, something needs to change. To take somebody's life the way she did, she should have done at least thirty years. Twelve years is nothing for Samantha's life and nothing for Callum who has lost his mum.'

8

Mistakes happen in all walks of life.

Whatever the sphere of human endeavour, there is always the capacity for something to go wrong. Most errors can be rectified without any permanent damage. Some have serious repercussions that last a long time. Other mistakes really are 'deadly' in every sense of the word.

And it was that type of blunder that enabled Anthony Joseph to be on the upper deck of a number 43 bus as it headed through north London at ten o'clock at night when he should have been under lock and key.

Joseph had been released from custody in Manchester just eight hours earlier, although he never should have been released. There was a warrant out for his arrest, but it wasn't put into effect, so he headed for London on a train and was there by nightfall. That was why Richard Whelan came to die. The night of 29 July 2005 had started out devoid of any threat, yet ended in the pointless death of a 28-year-old man. Richard Whelan, a hospitality agent who organised corporate events, had met his girlfriend Kerry Barker in Islington and gone for a Friday night drink with her. They decided to head towards her home in Muswell Hill for a meal. They were never to make it.

They boarded the bus in Islington at the same stop as hooded Joseph and went upstairs.

Also on the top deck was American Kelly Burke who was later to say that 23-year-old Joseph had 'a smirk' on his face and 'looked really weird'. Miss Barker noticed that the hooded young man was throwing chips at the American who was on her mobile phone to her husband – he wisely told her to go downstairs. She did, and that was when Joseph began to taunt the couple – who had endured fifteen minutes of his behaviour – a young man and woman who had never done him any harm in his life.

Then the nightmare began.

Miss Barker said: 'When she went downstairs I said, "He'd better not start throwing them at me, he's probably going to start throwing them at me."' She was then hit on the back of the head by a chip. 'It did take me by surprise. The man was laughing as he was throwing the chips, but there was nothing else really said.'

Mr Whelan got up to remonstrate with Joseph, little knowing the savage animal he was taking on, and a fight began. Legal secretary Kerry witnessed the savagery after her boyfriend had asked him to stop throwing the chips.

'Richard stood up, I turned around and they were fighting. The man was basically on top of Richard. Richard was trying to fight back, I remember trying to pull the man off. I was ringing the bell, I was screaming, "Leave him alone."'

As Joseph got up, she said, she saw a knife in his right hand and realised her boyfriend's shirt was soaked in blood. Other passengers described hearing a thumping sound from the upper deck and Barker screaming, 'Get off him, get off him. Oh my God, what's he doing? Make him stop.'

Another passenger, Jo Uttley, who was sitting on the lower deck, described hearing Barker's screams before Joseph came down the bus stairs. 'He just walked away down from the top deck with a gangster swagger as if it meant nothing to him. Some said he was grinning. He looked around the bus and demanded to be let off. He seemed to be unconnected to what happened. He behaved so calmly.'

Richard, from County Donegal, had been stabbed several times, including once through the heart. He staggered down the steps from the top deck, took his coat off and said, 'Look, he stabbed me' before collapsing. Miss Barker, thirty-eight, was at his side when he died in the Whittington Hospital in Highgate minutes later. He had been stabbed six times in the chest and torso.

A CCTV camera caught Joseph – who had been drinking spirits and taking crack cocaine – holding the knife above his head and biting Mr Whelan's hand as he tried to push him away. Time and time again he stabbed at the helpless passenger before escaping from the bus in the Holloway Road.

Miss Barker said of her partner: 'He was just a very private person, very calm, who got on well with people.'

Richard Whelan's sister Teresa Ward, thirty-seven, was also shocked by his needless death. 'There's no way anyone who hasn't been through what the family are going through right now can possibly imagine what it is like.' Describing him as 'a very gentle man', she said, 'What can you possibly say about something like this? He was just doing what any decent person would do, defending his girlfriend. He just wasn't the sort of person to get into any trouble. But then there was no fight, was there?'

She said the whole family was devastated including Mr Whelan's elderly father, who lived with Richard and who had lost his wife to cancer five years previously.

Only three weeks earlier, Richard's friend and fellow Arsenal fan, Ciaran Cassidy, was killed in the 7 July 2005 London bomb attacks and after the tragedy Richard had comforted the Cassidy family in their grief.

Veronica Cassidy, Mr Cassidy's mother, said: 'Richard was here from the moment Ciaran was missing and tried all he could for us, until the inevitable happened and he was confirmed as dead. Richard was a real support and what has happened to him is tragic.' Mr Cassidy, twenty-two, a shop worker from Finsbury Park, had been travelling on the Piccadilly line when he became one of the victims of the King's Cross bombers.

Although Joseph had escaped from the scene he was identified as the killer through DNA after detectives found his comb and a clump of his hair on the bus. Nearby he had dumped his leather jacket which was stained with Mr Whelan's blood. Six days after the attack he was arrested – a newspaper cutting about the stabbing and a folding knife were in his trouser pockets. He gave it to police telling them, 'You will find it anyway.'

He even asked a policeman: 'How many years do you get for murder?'

When forensic officers took clippings of his fingernails, Joseph said: 'I don't know why you want nail cuttings a week later. I've washed my hands loads of times since then.'

It was when Joseph appeared at the Old Bailey accused of murder in May 2007 that the timetable of events that led to his attack on Richard Whelan began to be made public.

Jonathan Turner, QC, prosecuting, described the stabbing on the bus and said there was no question that Anthony Joseph was the man who killed Richard Whelan.

But the defence would try to convince the jury that he was only guilty of manslaughter because of a mental abnormality, he said. The jury heard that Joseph had been released from Forest Bank prison in Manchester less than eight hours before the bus attack; he had been arrested after complaints from the head of a family in Surrey, only to be released after five weeks because of insufficient evidence.

'They had no option but to do that,' said Mr Turner. Joseph's view was that he had spent his time in custody for nothing.

'The consequence of that, the Crown say, is that he was an angry man who was released from prison.'

The court heard that Joseph had signed forms when he was arrested declaring that he had no mental illness, but later claimed to be a schizophrenic who heard voices.

Mr Turner said it was for the jury to decide whether Joseph was really insane, or 'an angry man with a bad temper in the habit of carrying a knife who used it to kill an unarmed man as a result of a stupid argument on a bus, knowing exactly what he was doing.'

But the jury couldn't decide and they were unable to reach a verdict. A retrial would be needed.

That meant that six months later Joseph was tried again, and on this occasion Victor Temple, QC, prosecuting, said, 'Mr Whelan was not prepared to sit down and do nothing. He got up and approached the defen-

Ben Kinsella, victim

Juress Kika and Jade Braithwaite, two of his killers

Kiyan Prince, victim

Dean Curtis, killer of
Kevin Johnson

Thomas Wood, killer of
Thomas Grant

Kodjo Yenga, victim

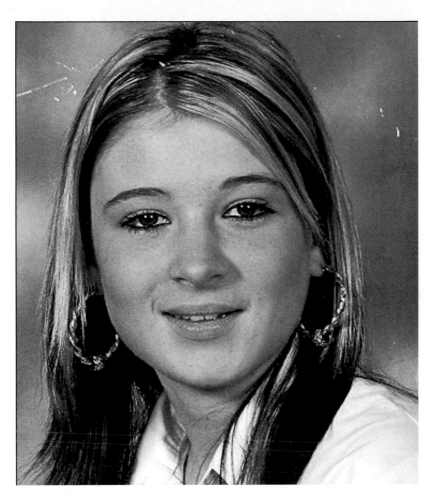

Samantha Madgin, victim

Daniel Pollen, victim

Michael Lynch, killer of
Daniel Pollen

Samantha Joseph, accomplice in the killing of Shakilus Townsend

David Idowu, victim

Rob Knox, victim

Karl Bishop, killer of
Rob Knox

dant. An altercation broke out which was between equals. The defendant, who habitually carried a knife, became verbally and physically aggressive. He took out the knife and stabbed the unarmed Mr Whelan in the top part of his body six or seven times. The defendant had been drinking and taking drugs and needed little or no excuse to turn his pent-up anger against the innocent victim.'

The new trial was also told by psychiatrist Dr Paul Chesterman that Joseph boasted how easy it was to fool doctors while being assessed after the attack. He also told the jury Joseph's actions could simply be explained by anger.

During the trials, however, a psychiatrist on behalf of the defence said that Joseph was being treated for paranoid schizophrenia in Broadmoor secure hospital. He thought Joseph had been suffering from the illness at the time of the killing and that his judgement had been impaired by it. Joseph, he said, also appeared to have the start of a personality disorder and told doctors he had acted in self-defence.

Mr Philip Katz, defending, said Joseph was suffering from the onset of schizophrenia at the time of the killing.

The jury were hearing conflicting views from experts and after the second jury also failed to agree on a verdict Joseph pleaded guilty to manslaughter on the grounds of diminished responsibility. The Crown decided not to go ahead with a third murder trial.

Afterwards, Whelan's sister Teresa had her own verdict on the man who had killed her brother. 'We feel the defence of diminished responsibility has been used as a defence for the un-defendable, with so much evidence showing that Anthony Joseph was an angry and vindictive man. He has tried to excuse his actions by claiming mental illness. In our opinion, he callously killed Richard for no reason at all.'

She described her brother as 'a very private, quiet man brought up with high values who treated people with respect. Our lives are changed for ever. We miss Richard every day, his gentleness, his kindness and his love, and we will always miss him in a way that is so painful we cannot put it into words.'

She said Richard, had 'made the mistake of judging another by his own standards'.

No sooner was Joseph's manslaughter plea accepted than the full, shocking details of how he came to be freed to be on that bus – drunk, fuelled by drugs and armed with a knife – began to emerge.

Joseph had been mistakenly released from the young offenders' institution in Manchester after charges of abduction and unlawful sex with a fifteen-year-old were dropped. Because of a separate arrest warrant, issued after Joseph failed to attend court in Liverpool four weeks before the killing on charges of burglary, he should have been retained in custody, but was instead released in error.

Eight hours after his release he killed Mr Whelan in what was described by Detective Chief Inspector John Macdonald, who led the investigation, as a horrendous attack.

Merseyside police said that the force had followed the correct guidelines and circulated Joseph's details on the national police computer as soon he failed to appear in court. A government spokeswoman said ministers from the Home Office and Ministry of Justice, along with the Solicitor-General, had written to 'chief inspectors of the Crown Prosecution Service, court administration, constabulary and prisons to gain a full understanding of what happened in June and July 2005, and to make sure that any mistakes that may have occurred do not happen again'.

The next month, December 2007, Joseph, twenty-three, was sentenced to an indefinite period in Broadmoor and Mr Justice Gross said: 'The circumstances of this case are tragic indeed. They form the nightmare of all those who use public transport.'

The judge said Mr Whelan's reaction had been 'entirely understandable and, for that matter, praiseworthy'. He told Joseph: 'You should not have been released at all. This is a matter for concern. You bear considerable responsibility for your actions which were fuelled by alcohol and crack cocaine.'

Eventually in April 2008 came the Solicitor-General's report into the events that led to Mr Whelan's death by knife in the hands of a madman – and it was damning. The report, conducted by inspectors from the Crown Prosecution Service, police and courts, condemned the lax attitude within the justice system, particularly in relation to bail. Joseph had been repeatedly bailed to an address in Camden, north London, by magistrates in both London and Liverpool, where he was arrested for burglary in April 2005. The address did not exist and the report found no evidence that the authorities had checked its veracity. 'There seems to be too ready an acceptance of the commission of offences while on bail, insufficient rigour in respect of checking the validity of proposed bail conditions, and an apparent acceptance of the continual breach of bail conditions', it said.

It highlighted the fact that only forty-six prisons out of 140 in England and Wales at that time had access to the Police National Computer, and called for far more widespread links. It said the same recommendation was made in 2006 by the inquiry into the racist murder of inmate Zahid Mubarek at Feltham young offenders' institution.

The prison service had requested extended access but was still awaiting a response, the report said, and gave a succession of examples where information about Joseph was incomplete or not correctly passed between different agencies.

'We have to conclude that throughout the various

court hearings, the approach to the verification of bail conditions to assure the magistrates that they could safely bail the defendant was lacking in rigour', it said.

Joseph had nine convictions in the four years before the killing, though none was for violence. The report said: 'We have found nothing to suggest that the criminal justice agencies should have been aware that the defendant was likely to commit an offence of extreme violence or that he was suffering from an extreme mental illness. However, what we have found is what may best be described as a lackadaisical or nonchalant approach within the criminal justice system to many routine aspects of the handling of cases.

'The lack of diligence in verifying suggested bail conditions, scant evidence of enforcement of those conditions and a failure to deal effectively with breaches when they occurred, all contributed to events taking the course they did. This was compounded by a lack of communication between the agencies in the various parts of the country.'

Shadow justice secretary Nick Herbert said the report was a damning indictment of complacency towards bail.

'It is also a further tragic example of how the government's IT failures in the criminal justice system have put members of the public at risk. Reform is needed so that bail conditions are properly enforced and defendants know that breaches will result in immediate action.'

Sandra Sullivan, of the charity Victims' Voice, whose daughter was killed by a schizophrenic woman, said: 'I hate it when people say lessons will be learned. This kind of criminal behaviour is repetitive and predictable. I want to see accountability when things go wrong.'

In January 2009 came the announcement that police forces in England and Wales were to be issued with new guidance on identifying and managing risks after the 'culture of complacency' report, a cross-agency working group said. The guidance, to be published later in the year, would enable police 'to better manage risk, particularly around violent individuals and situations' and would include 'practical advice' relating to bail applications.

The January report by the group was set up to implement the recommendations of an official investigation into Mr Whelan's death.

Solicitor-General Vera Baird, QC, said a number of the previous year's report recommendations 'have now been implemented in full and significant work has been conducted on those remaining'.

The working group said new guidance would be issued to police forces, and found that 'where bail is granted, the verification of addresses put forward for bail purposes, both as to their accuracy and their continuing suitability, needs to be pursued above all on a proportionate basis, depending on the assessment of the risk posed by the defendant'.

The group also looked at giving prisons greater access to the Police National Computer, but a pilot scheme at London's Pentonville prison had only limited success and 'could have created an ambiguity around which agency would be responsible for cross-referencing police and prison records'.

Instead, the group said that 'police access to prison data should negate the need for prisons themselves to safeguard against inadvertent release'.

Police forces were also told to alter their procedures to prevent so-called predictive resulting, where custody officers update their systems with expected outcomes of court hearings in a bid to 'progress their paperwork'.

Exactly how well these recommendations work, only time will tell.

One thing that is certain, however, is that 'the system' failed poor, innocent Richard Whelan in a terrifying and irreversible manner that night on the number 43 bus.

9

Closed-circuit television is the Big Brother that is watching us all today.

No nation is observed more than the British. Nowhere seems out of bounds for the all-seeing eye of the cameras. They are, depending on your point of view, an invaluable tool in the fight to keep law and order in our public places, or an affront to the right to privacy that every citizen should have.

No one knows exactly how many there are: some say over four million – one for approximately every fifteen people on the island. If you are out and about on the streets and transport systems of London you may be captured on no fewer than 300 cameras in one day.

There is also a dispute over their effectiveness. Hundreds of millions are spent every year on installing, maintaining and monitoring them, and yet they are said to help solve just 3 per cent of crimes. That money could be spent more effectively and with better results, maintain critics.

Yet of all the countless images caught in the camera's omnipercipient eye, few, if any, can be as chilling as the ones frozen in time in the Brewery shopping centre car park at Romford in Essex. They were to be shown to millions later, capturing for ever the terrible moment when a young man's life was lost.

It was shortly after 2.30 a.m. on 8 July 2005 and Daniel Pollen, a twenty-year-old media and cultural studies student at Southampton Solent University, was waiting for a lift with his best friend Andrew Griffiths. It had been Andy's twentieth birthday and the pair of them were leaning against bicycle racks waiting for Daniel's teenage sister Kirsty to pick them up.

Three young men swaggered into view from around a corner. Like the pair they approached, they too had been in the Time and Envy nightclub, although the two groups had not encountered each other there. They sauntered towards the two innocent friends and, without any warning or provocation, launched a savage attack lasting just over one minute. Unsuspecting Andrew was the first to suffer, receiving a swinging punch to the head, and collapsing to the ground. Daniel was then chased by a knife-wielding member of the trio, his jaw broken with a blow, and then he was stabbed in the heart, collapsing with a two-inch hole in his chest, never to regain consciousness. The savage who had thrust the blade into him then returned to stricken Andrew and stabbed him several times. Andrew, a medical student at Durham University, was left lying in a pool of blood, but miraculously lived to tell the tale. The three attackers calmly walked to their car and drove off. It was all over as quickly as that.

The call every parent dreads came shortly afterwards when Daniel's sister Kirsty rang their mother Josie to tell her that her son had been stabbed.

The thoughts that ran through the mother's head were the obvious ones: 'When your daughter is calling at 2.30 a.m. to say that your son has been stabbed . . . well, then it's really bad. I was immediately saying, "He's going to be all right." I asked if she'd phoned for an ambulance, I told her to stem the flow of blood, to get a wad of material and press it to him. I asked her to tell us where she was. There were three further phone calls from Kirsty. On the third, she said, "Mum, he's making a funny noise." I told her to put the phone to his ear and I started praying for him. I said, "Daniel, hold on. Just hold on."'

The area had been taped off by police by the time Mrs Pollen arrived on the scene. She lifted the tape and ran towards her son, telling a police officer that she was his mother as she approached. 'They were resuscitating him, and all I could see were his long legs.'

The attack had been captured on the area's CCTV and

within hours police had tracked the attackers down to the home of sixteen-year-old Michael Lynch of Stratford in east London. He and his two cronies, decorators Timmy Sullivan from Barking and Michael Onokah from Ilford, raced out of the back as the police came in the front. Lynch remained at liberty for three days, although the other two were arrested not long afterwards.

At first, Lynch, a father of two, could not be identified because of his age, but eventually he was named when he and the others appeared at Woolwich Crown Court and Judge Shirley Anwyl, QC, said the murder of Daniel and the intentional wounding of Andrew, which he had admitted, were so serious that the anonymity he had enjoyed so far should be lifted.

Sullivan and Onokah had been acquitted of the murder at a three-week trial, but were convicted of causing Daniel gricvous bodily harm with intent and intentionally wounding Andrew.

Yet why the trio launched their attack on two innocent young men was still a mystery.

Before the sentences were passed, prosecutor Christopher Kinch told the court that even after the trial that had taken place 'we are no nearer any clear explanation for the unleashing of that gratuitous violence on two entirely innocent young men.'

The judge said to Lynch: 'This was a coordinated, calculated attack that was as brutal as it was senseless. Mr Pollen and Mr Griffiths had done nothing to upset, antagonise or provoke any of you defendants. They just happened to be in the wrong place at the wrong time.'

Lynch had previous convictions for violence – including shooting an Asian man in the leg with a ball-bearing gun and racially abusing him – and was on bail for burglary at the time of the attack. The judge added: 'This attack occurred late at night in a deserted car park. There was no one there who could come to their aid. You approached them from behind, taking them by complete surprise. The general public is concerned, and rightly so, by the violent use of knives, and when a knife is used and fatal or serious injury is caused, the court must impose a severe sentence.'

Lynch received a life sentence for the murder and although life imprisonment was mandatory, when considering his genuine remorse, the judge said in view of the fact that he had not meant to kill anyone, his low IQ and other problems in life, and the pain and suffering his incarceration would cause to his 'very young family', she had reduced what would have been a recommended minimum of twenty-four years in prison to one of fifteen before parole could be considered.

She added: 'If it remains necessary for the protection of the public you will continue to be detained.'

Onokah had a number of previous convictions, two of them for robbery, and was on parole for one of them the night he helped attack the two students. The judge said that while she accepted the remorse he had expressed was genuine, she had no doubt he posed a 'high risk' to the public in future and so she passed an indeterminate sentence with the minimum term he would have to serve fixed at five years.

A similar sentence was imposed on Sullivan (who was on the run from the police at the time) who threw the first punch and then acted as getaway driver.

Before sentence was passed, one national newspaper had called on the judge to jail all three young men for life, and a petition bearing 50,000 signatures supporting that move was handed in at Downing Street.

Andrew's mother Sandra said: 'I'm delighted that so many people have signed it. What these boys did to Daniel and Andrew is horrific – they should get life.

'It has really affected Andrew but I feel incredibly lucky to have him here with me. It could easily have been me who was grieving instead of the Pollen family.'

She also called for more to be done on the issue of knife crime. 'Unfortunately, this type of thing happens all the time. Until people start standing up to say "No", there will be other families like the Pollens who will have to mourn.'

Daniel's parents, Terry and Josie Pollen, suffered the torment of all parents who had lost a son in such a manner. 'The verdicts and sentences imposed today can only provide us with a measure of justice, as Daniel's killer could be free in some fifteen years. This surely must be a concern for us all. Harsher sentences must be imposed that create a real deterrent to the casual possession and use of a knife, then no more innocent lives will be lost. The present situation we feel is unacceptable.

'We leave court today trying to rebuild our lives, with only the treasured memories of Daniel.'

They also paid tribute to their 'kind, loving, funny, and intelligent' son who was 'loved and liked by all. We are deeply proud of our son, confident that neither his actions nor Andrew's caused or contributed to the violent and brutal assault perpetrated by the three assailants.'

Josie added later, 'They said in the witness box they'd gone out to enjoy themselves. They felt it was their human right to attack Daniel and Andy as part of their evening's entertainment. Well what about Daniel's and Andy's human right to sit and wait for Kirsty without being attacked? I don't agree that they were in the wrong place at the wrong time. We all have a right to walk our streets and be safe.

'Sentences get reduced. It's almost like supermarket sentencing: buy one, get one free; buy one, get one half-price; serve half-a-sentence and get one free. I want to see them serve their full sentence. That's what they are there to serve. Why take half of it off? Why? Where does that come from? I believe there's a chain of responsibility that starts with the parents and ends with the government and the criminal justice system, which are there to protect us. Their priority should be protecting the general public. So far, it hasn't been that. There has been more concern for the criminal, making sentences as short as possible. One of the reasons they give is overcrowding in prisons. The answer is simple: build more prisons.'

Andrew Griffiths, the survivor of that terrible encounter, also called for a change in the law, with tougher penalties for those caught carrying knives.

'Knives can and do destroy lives. The police can only do so much; the law has to change, to make it a more serious offence to carry a knife, with punishments reflecting the associated gruesome crimes. Because of a knife my life will never be the same again; they have taken my best friend from me.'

He described the attack on them as 'pointless', 'motiveless' and 'brutal'.

'In a seventy-second frenzy, three people, who we had never had any contact with before, stabbed Dan in the heart and wounded me twice, they ran off leaving us disabled on the floor. I have never and will never understand the need for anyone to carry knives. I have many friends and they don't feel the need to do so. A friend can never be someone who carries a knife. The effect of Dan's murder is like throwing a stone in a pond, the ripples never end; it has affected so many different people and will continue to do so. I am making a box with memories of Dan in. In some small way this will keep him with me for ever.

'I didn't even see any of the gang approach us and the first I knew they were there was when I got this terrible blow. I was knocked out for a couple of seconds and I fell to the floor. This punch broke my jaw. I saw Dan's arm reach out to try and protect me – an act that I will never forget. This is when Lynch punched Dan for the first time.

'There was just no reason for it. I just want some reason, any reason, for why this happened. If they are prepared to take a life they should be prepared to serve life. The law has to change.'

Detective Chief Inspector Dave Brown, who led the investigation, said the reasons for the 'heinous' and 'unwarranted' attack were still unclear.

But he said: 'What is apparent is the effect of carrying knives; in this instance it resulted in the tragic, unnecessary murder of a young man. If your child, friend, partner or associates carry a knife this cannot be warranted. Carrying knives is illegal and possession can see you serve a four-year prison sentence.

'This has to be the most violent and unwarranted attack I have ever dealt with in thirty years. It was completely unprovoked and to this day we're still unclear as to what the actual motive was.'

Although the court heard of the gang's remorse, Mr Brown said that while in custody and during questioning 'they offered no defence and showed no signs of remorse.' He added: 'They made no comment, they never told us anything about why they chose to attack Daniel and Andrew in that way.'

Mr Brown said the CCTV images had been released to the public in consultation with the families to send a message about the consequences of carrying and using a knife. 'It's also important that people understand if they do act in this manner it will be caught on CCTV and it will be used in evidence,' he said.

All knife crime is horrific. The damage a sharp blade can do to the human body is sickening and threatens the right of people to walk the streets without fear. These were among the factors that inspired Daniel Pollen's parents to allow the footage of the attack, the film that had been instrumental in the rapid arrest of the three attackers, to be shown on television.

'It was a very hard decision,' Mrs Pollen said. 'We were asked by the police to release it to highlight how CCTV can monitor criminal activity. It was also felt it shows the harsh reality of knife crime in this country. It was a motiveless attack and the reality is that it could have been anyone's son. The first time I watched the film, I just wanted to see him alive. As a mother, you want to be able to look after your child. Seeing the attack and knowing I couldn't stop it, that I couldn't make it all right for him, was the most awful thing.'

A month after the sentencing of the trio of thugs, and a year after Daniel's death, the Pollens were among six families, all victims of knife crime, who met the Lord Chancellor, Lord Falconer, to call for longer sentences for those who carried knives, and twenty-five years' imprisonment for knife murderers. Lord Falconer was moved to tears when he read a note about the knifing to death of headmaster Philip Lawrence that the doomed young man had written when he was just ten. In a class exercise, Daniel had written to 'The Past' and said: 'Because you made guns and knives people are murdered every day. An example is a headmaster stabbed defending a pupil. If you hadn't made guns and knives that headmaster would still be alive and so would other people.'

The pictures of the attack shown on television had a profound effect on those who saw them. Many viewers felt compelled to write to Daniel's family or post their feelings on the internet.

One woman, who had never met Daniel or his family, summed up the feelings of everyone who saw those fuzzy, distant images. In a letter she said:

I felt compelled to write this:

I watched in horror and cried when I saw this vile and obscene murder. I wish I hadn't watched it as it has really upset and disturbed me and I feel physically sick to think that these two young men were minding their own business and innocently waiting on a lift home after a night out and for no reason were attacked by these evil, vile, scum.

I am a mother of two lovely teenage boys! One of them is not unlike Daniel and I feel angry that these people have only had jail sentences when they should be hanged for what they've done.

I am a peaceful, law-abiding citizen and I don't say that lightly. Nothing is being done in this country to deter these monsters. It's about time for some real justice to be meted out and apart from anything else it would take this scum off the streets and ensure that they never put another family through this nightmare.

Thank you to Daniel's family for allowing this to be screened. This should be taken around every High School in the Country.

I can't imagine how Andrew must be feeling and can only send my love and prayers to him and his family.

My deepest sympathies to Daniel's family.

God Bless you all.

Daniel RIP.

10

It was almost 11.26 p.m. on a cold Thursday night in January 2006 when solicitor Tom ap Rhys Pryce walked out of brightly lit Kensal Green tube station in north London. He wore a suit and an overcoat and under his arm was a briefcase as he went through the ticket barrier, captured on Camera 15 of the station's closed-circuit television system. He had told his fiancée, fellow lawyer Adele Eastman, he would be home by 11.30 that night, and he was on schedule as the house he shared with her was just a few minutes' walk away.

'Home' was in Bathurst Gardens, bought two years earlier for £234,000. One of those countless streets of small terraced houses built by the Victorians and which, in recent years, had become home to many young professionals unable to afford the exorbitant prices of more fashionable – and supposedly safer – parts of the city.

Many of the young professionals were children of the

provinces and so Kensal Green, for all its faults, had become a stepping-stone for them on their way to larger, more comfortable homes in the years to come.

Tom ap Rhys Pryce seemed to fit the bill in that respect. He was born into a distinguished military family. His great-grandfather, General Sir Henry Edward ap Rhys Pryce, an aide-de-camp to King George VI, was awarded the DSO in the First World War and mentioned in despatches seven times. His great-great-uncle, Major Caryl ap Rhys Pryce, also awarded the DSO in the First World War, had previously led an anarchist uprising in Mexico in 1911.

Tom had been born in Broxbourne, Hertfordshire, and had spent some of his childhood in Africa before returning to the UK. At thirteen he won a music and academic scholarship to Marlborough College public school in Wiltshire whose alumni include poet John Betjeman, singer Chris de Burgh, actor Wilfred Hyde-White and the Queen's granddaughter Princess Eugenie.

He passed grade eight violin and achieved top grades in his Greek, Latin and English A levels to win a place at Trinity College, Cambridge, where he took a first in classics which he followed with a masters degree in the subject.

After four years of studying classics, he decided to become a lawyer and earned a diploma in law from City University, London, followed by a year at Nottingham Trent University, where he was awarded his diploma in legal practice in 1999. The following year he joined the top City law firm Linklaters.

As he left the comparative safety of the tube station that night all those plans he, and those who loved him, held were doomed. Less than an hour earlier he had telephoned his fiancée to say that he was on his way home from a function in the City of London ... but he would never make it. Within minutes he would be dead, his belongings – gloves, a book and some documents, including plans for his September wedding reception at a local gastro-pub and then a Tuscan honeymoon – scattered along the street where he lived. So was his blood from the two fatal stab wounds to his chest and the other injuries to his thigh, head and hands that had ended his life.

Residents of the road heard the noise of the struggle at 11.44 p.m. and telephoned the police immediately. The attack on him had begun by number 56 and near number 82 there was blood on a parked Audi. Outside number 86 there was blood on a tree and one of his gloves on the pavement alongside his documents. It was outside number 90 that he collapsed, saying to his attackers who had trailed him from the station, 'That's everything, you've got everything.' By the time police arrived his two attackers had disappeared into the night taking their gains with them: an Oyster card, a mobile phone and twenty pounds in cash.

It was a crime that shocked the nation. When the events that led to his death and the culture that had bred his killers eventually became known it was, if anything, more horrifying . . .

Delano Brown and Donnel Carty's backgrounds lacked the achievements of Tom ap Rhys Pryce but they did not come from lives of utter deprivation. True, their mothers had separated from their fathers when they were young, but both boys had a relationship with their fathers and both were raised as churchgoers. They had met a decade earlier, when they were eight, at the nearby Kensal Green church where their families worshipped.

Carty's mother, Barbara Prince, was not even eighteen when she gave birth to him, and as he grew up she found it hard to cope. Young Donnel went to stay with his father Marcus, but chose to leave because Marcus was 'too strict'. Next stop was his grandparents, not far from Bathurst Gardens, but he spent more and more time with his uncle, Clive Carty. It was to his house in Kilburn that the two boys would run after killing ap Rhys Pryce.

Carty at one stage went to a local youth charity which helped find employment for young people in the neighbourhood and, because his reading and writing were poor, the centre referred him to a literacy course at a local college. He chose not to attend, however, although he did go to a music production course. One of the tracks that he produced chillingly contained lyrics boasting of his willingness to stab someone.

Delano Brown spent time in Kensal Green with his godfather and grandparents, although he grew up with his mother Maureen Leo and two sisters in nearby Sudbury in Middlesex.

His mother had a full-time job working in the catering department of the Metropolitan Police, so the responsibility of cooking for his two sisters and walking them to school fell on his shoulders. He was a good footballer and worked part-time in a sports centre in addition to passing GCSEs in English, maths and PE. Once he left school he completed a course at Uxbridge College that qualified him to teach sport to children. He then worked for a period at his godfather's construction business.

While they were growing up the two young 'cousins' had drifted apart for a while, but they started seeing each other again, and Brown was eager to please his 'harder' childhood pal.

If the glittering prizes that beckoned for Tom were never going to be within the reach of Brown and Carty, there was also another side to both these young men that was to show the base level to which they were soon to descend.

By December 2005 Carty was eighteen and Brown seventeen. But Carty was now known as 'Armani' and

Brown was 'Shy', both important members of the local KG Tribe gang they had become part of. The gang specialised in 'steaming' – racing onto crowded tubes to target commuters for their wallets, purses, cash and valuables – and if their helpless victims resisted they would be stabbed, 'juked' in the gang's language, normally in the leg.

In a seven-month period their daring and violence escalated and they carried out an estimated 150 crimes in this brutal, cowardly manner, on the Underground, mainline rail networks and the streets. A fifth of all the robberies carried out on the 250 miles of Underground that year were their work and the gang were getting out of control.

They used a map of the Underground not to find their way from station to station but to construct their own 'good muggers' guide'. The map was pinned to the bedroom wall of another of the gang members, nineteen-year-old Aaron Dennis, known as 'Red Rat', and he highlighted with a red pen the best areas, or 'Eats', to strike: Hyde Park Corner and Queensway were shown as the best places to snatch Rolex watches, and Camden Town and Colindale on the Northern line as hotspots for tube muggings.

At Neasden and Sudbury Town Dennis wrote 'Beef', indicating he got into gang fights in those areas, while the districts he felt secure in were called 'Endz'. Westbourne Park had a significant police presence, so he called it 'hot' and he changed pens to mark in black alongside Hillingdon the words 'Got Nicked'.

Dennis was involved in several stabbings and, only the night before the murder of Mr ap Rhys Pryce, he left a civil servant for dead on the Metropolitan line near Pinner and another man was stabbed with a kitchen blade on the Hammersmith & City line.

The gang ran riot, attacking passengers on five tube lines – the Northern, Jubilee, Bakerloo, Hammersmith & City and Central – across nine boroughs, and on 23 December alone they targeted five tube trains, carrying out ten violent muggings and two stabbings.

Since 2004, in juvenile and other courts, gang members had been given between them almost six years' worth of supervision orders, conditional discharges, referral orders, action plans and training orders – for offences including causing grievous bodily harm to a police officer, robbery and burglary. Detectives were to say at least four of the gang were 'killers in the making'.

The gang lived outside any civilised code of behaviour, their only status within their own society was violence; the greater the violence, the greater their standing in the eyes of others. There was an air of tragic, horrific inevitability about the end of this reign of terror.

Carty and Brown had been busy the night of Tom's death. They got off a northbound Bakerloo line train at Kensal Green at just after 11 p.m. and fled the station about five minutes later, after claiming their first victim of the night.

Their hoods over their heads, they had approached restaurant chef Kurshid Ali, who was sitting down on a bench on the platform, and stole his mobile phone, cash and travel cards before running out of the station at 11.07 p.m.

The victim reported the robbery to staff, who took his name, but he did not want the matter reported to police and it was only when detectives hunting the killers asked British Transport Police whether there had been any recent robberies at the station that the incident came to light.

Mr Ali could not have known just how lucky he was to emerge alive from the attack.

Afterwards he admitted: 'I was so very frightened. I didn't move at all. I just let them do what they wanted. When I think about them, I can't really tell them apart. The fear made them merge into one. When you think about what happened to the other man, I know I was very lucky. They were very violent. They just stood in front of me and didn't even bother to hide their faces. I didn't see a weapon, but I knew they had one.'

Moments later they were lounging outside a convenience store when they spotted the smartly dressed ap Rhys Pryce walking past. Carty whistled at Brown and the pair began to follow him along Bathurst Gardens.

The exact reason they decided to kill the lawyer may

never be known, but the irresistible conclusion is that he chose to 'fight back'. He didn't look 'streetwise', they reckoned he would be easy pickings. They didn't expect a fight as he was a classic victim for them: a white, respectable, besuited man, not the sort to give them any trouble. It was a terrible mistake on his part, but an understandable one to make. Why should he submit to their threats, after all? Perhaps they just wanted to attack him 'for kicks'.

Anique Bazil was at her computer at her home in Bathurst Gardens when she heard the sound of running and looked out of her window to see Tom trying to escape his attackers. She later recalled that he finally gave up, handed over something and then collapsed: 'I saw a white man running, with two black men following closely behind him. The black men were a couple of paces behind. They caught up to him. They stopped near a tree. He turned to face them. There was a struggle. He stepped into the road and they followed him. There was a struggle. It was not a fight. The man was trying to defend himself. He was trying to block them, to try to keep them away from him. They were trying to take something from him. They moved between parked vehicles. The white man went first, trying to get away from them, and they went after him and there was a struggle in the road. I think I remember him just giving up and handing something over. They grabbed whatever it was and they walked away. The man walked.

He was staggering and fell. He got up and walked a few paces and fell behind a van. I did not see him again.'

Appalling as the attack was, the lack of remorse shown by the killers somehow made it worse.

A few minutes after they left him lying, dying in the street, Carty phoned a girlfriend using the lawyer's mobile phone. He didn't care, or know, that the call would be traced. There was even more bravado to come. The next morning, even as police were in the area, Carty walked from his grandparents' home towards the crime scene and sold the phone to a shopkeeper at the end of Bathurst Gardens. Police were just yards away.

The murder dominated the news for days to come. It was one of the pivotal crimes of its time, illustrating as it did, even before anyone was arrested, the gulf between the two societies it represented: one hard-working and respectable, the other feral, callous and bloodthirsty.

A mere twelve hours after the attack on Tom the media was being briefed about his death, which was described by a detective as 'a particularly vicious and gratuitous attack', and the photograph of him that was to sear its way into the public conscience was issued.

For three days running, police released new CCTV images in the hunt for the killers, including those poignant final pictures of Tom leaving Kensal Green station on the short walk to his home after a night out. It was a fast-moving investigation with new clues developing almost every few hours. The words of sorrow from those who knew Tom were to add to the emotion of the case when his parents John and Estella from Weybridge in Surrey said: 'Words cannot express our sense of loss and sadness at what has happened – he will be hugely missed by everyone who knew him.' They added that their son was a 'unique and beautiful person' who could not wait to get married. 'We appeal to anyone with any information that may help solve this senseless crime which cut short the life of a gifted young man who had everything to live for to come forward.'

The father of Tom's fiancée, Rod Eastman, added that the entire family had been heartbroken by his death. 'Adele had rung me only hours before. She was cooking a hot meal for them both because Tom was expected home any minute,' said Mr Eastman, from Bishops Nympton, Devon. 'But the next time she spoke to me, early on Friday morning, it was to tell me he was dead. We're all numb and need time to take this all in. He was a lovely lad. Obviously, Adele is beside herself.

'Tom and Adele were so looking forward to the wedding,' he added. 'They both loved Italy and wanted a really special occasion. Everything was booked. Now it isn't going to happen and it's impossible to describe that feeling.'

Even as those words were being spoken, the net was tightening around Carty and Brown, whose arrogance and stupidity was to contribute to their arrest.

They had been captured on CCTV escaping from the station after robbing Mr Ali, and two neighbours who saw the attack on Tom described the robbers as young black men wearing the hoods of their jackets over their heads. As well as using the mobile phone of the dead man they also used Mr Ali's mobile to call a girlfriend. And, in addition to selling Mr ap Rhys Pryce's mobile the next morning for thirty pounds, Carty had also been photographed trying to use the dead man's Oyster card – a pre-paid electronic card for use on transport in London – at Kensal Green station on the same day.

Six days after the attack the inevitable happened and Carty and Brown were arrested. Initially they both denied being involved: Carty was to tell police a practically unbelievable story that he had bought the phone the previous night from two men as he walked to catch a bus and that he had found the Oyster card on a wall.

They both denied murder when they eventually appeared at the Old Bailey on 31 October that year and the chilling events of that night were relived again in detail by prosecutor Richard Horwell, QC: 'The motive was greed. He was being targeted as the victim of a robbery. He had just left the Underground system and he appeared rightly as if he was on his way home from work and he was likely to have something worth stealing.' It was 'two against one' he said, adding: 'They were armed and, of course, he was not. It did not matter to them that this man had worked hard for his position in life, that he had a promising career in the legal system ahead of him. It did not matter that he was to marry in September. All that was best in life was ahead of him but to them he was no more than a means to an end, and they treated him accordingly. Tom ap Rhys Pryce was a proud man and there is a real prospect that he did not submit to the demands of the robbers. He may well have taken them on and if he did, the robbers rose to the challenge and they proceeded in their attack on him.'

He added: 'What value did the robbers place on his life? Their reward was Mr ap Rhys Pryce's Oyster card, his bank cards, driving licence and mobile phone.'

'That night, the police had very little to work on but, as the investigation continued, it became clear that the two defendants were the two robbers. The police discovered that they were members of a team of robbers who stabbed two victims during the course of robberies three weeks before.'

After describing the attack on Mr Ali he said: 'We suggest that the two defendants had not completed their business that night and that, within such a short time of the robbery on Mr Ali, they ambushed this man obviously on his way home from work.'

Mr Horwell said the men continued the attack 'as if the use of a knife was an inevitable event once resistance had been demonstrated'.

When the defendants were arrested six days after the murder, both were said to have given false alibis. Brown later admitted robbing Mr ap Rhys Pryce but said it was Carty who had knifed him. The charge of robbery was denied by Carty. They both pleaded guilty to the robbery of Mr Ali and to conspiracy to rob in December, but denied charges of wounding the two victims with intent to cause grievous bodily harm.

Mr Horwell said: 'They knew there was a knife. They knew it might be used. They did not care about their victims – only themselves.'

Despite their protestations of innocence, with each blaming the other, the evidence against the evil pair was overwhelming and they were both found guilty of murder and jailed for life, although the jury deliberated for three days before returning their verdict.

They were also found guilty of wounding two other victims with intent and causing grievous bodily harm. And they had, at least, admitted robbing Mr Ali and conspiracy to rob in December.

Mr Justice Aikens told the killers: 'Tom ap Rhys Pryce had the grave misfortune to be in the wrong place at just the wrong time. He was true to his nature – he was not going to let two young thugs rob him in the street where he lived. In having the courage to resist he paid with his life.'

Horrific as his death had been, the reaction of Tom's family and loved ones emphasised the tragedy even more.

His fiancée Adele Eastman made a victim impact

statement the power and raw emotion of which had never been heard in an English court before.

It had to be read by prosecutor Richard Horwell, QC, as she was not allowed to address the court in person. Perhaps that might have diminished its power, but when read and heard by a larger audience afterwards it was a moving and eloquent summary of the events that bleak night in north-west London. For that reason alone it is worth repeating virtually in full, both for its emotion from a woman talking of a lost loved one and for the pinpoint accuracy she brings to her assessment of the impact the bloodthirsty use of a knife can have on a civilised society. It brought tears to the eyes of many in court, including Miss Eastman, as she listened to her own words read by another. Only Carty and Brown seemed unmoved.

Even now it is hard to read without feeling her pain. She said:

My name is Adele Eastman. I am the fiancée of Tom ap Rhys Pryce.

I have been invited to make a statement on the impact that Tom's murder on 12th January of this year has had on me.

I had hoped I might be able to read my statement from the witness box in open court. I wanted Carty and Brown to hear directly from me the absolute devastation which they have caused.

I must start by saying that my sense of pain and horror at losing Tom, and in such a brutal way, is literally indescribable.

I have found it almost impossible even to try to put it into words, but hope that I manage to convey it at least to some extent through my statement.

Tom was determined from an early age to reach his full potential in life. He worked incredibly hard and made the most of every opportunity available to him.

He gave his best in everything he did and he succeeded. Yet, despite his many achievements, he was the most humble person I have ever known.

In a message left on the tree next to where he died, a friend of ours wrote: 'I remember sitting next to you at our friend's wedding, standing to sing the first hymn, and looking in wonder at you as this pure, amazing voice came out . . . I had no idea, after so many years of knowing you, how beautifully you sang. You were often like that – quietly achieving all these amazing things.'

There was still so much more that Tom wanted to achieve and to experience. I grieve for his loss of life and for my loss of him. Tom was my best friend, my soulmate.

I adored him – I always will. I miss him more than I could ever describe: his beautiful heart, his brilliant mind, his big loving eyes, his gentle voice, his gleeful laugh and quirky sense of humour, his dancing, our chats, and the great fun that we used to have together. I miss us. We had been together for four years when last October Tom asked me to marry him. It was the most beautiful moment of my life.

I said yes immediately, through tears of joy. We were deeply in love and blissfully happy together.

One of our friends wrote in his letter of condolence to me: 'The love between you was so infectious. It radiated outward and filled everyone around with warmth.' Our plans for our wedding, which was due to be held in Italy in September this year, were going so well and, as with everything, Tom and I planned it together. We were so excited. The period of our engagement (just three short months) was the happiest time of our lives. On the day Tom was killed he had made contact with the priest who was due to conduct our wedding ceremony.

He printed off the details he had received that afternoon, together with his wedding vows. They were found later that night strewn around him on the pavement as the paramedics battled to save his life.

We had felt that the best was yet to come: our wedding, children, and a long and happy marriage. But it was all only ever to be a dream.

As I ran in and out of our home that night over a period of hours, frantic for news of Tom, as I received the news of his death, as I lay convulsing in shock, Carty and Brown were chatting to their girlfriends on Tom's and another stolen mobile telephone.

The day after Tom's murder, a friend kindly cancelled the appointment I had made to show my mother what would have been my wedding dress.

We then had to wait for a couple of days before being able to identify Tom's body. I could not do it. I could not bear to see Tom dead.

I wanted our last memory of each other to be the same – the wonderful goodbye we had had on the Thursday morning at the train station.

In a matter of seconds wedding plans and a future together had changed to funeral plans and a lifetime apart.

I will never forget the complete confusion of Tom's three-year-old niece on the day of his funeral: one day being swung through the air and chased around the garden by her beloved Uncle Thomas; the next, there were no more games, there was no more laughter – only tears.

As she sat quietly by his graveside, her little hands gripping hold of the edge, we watched her Uncle Thomas being gently lowered in a 'big box' into the ground.

If there was anything left of my heart to break, it broke in that moment.

The pain is unlike anything I have ever experienced and unlike anything I could have ever imagined.

I feel as though Carty and Brown have ripped out my heart with their bare hands and torn it, very slowly, into pieces. Witnessing the pain that our families and friends are also suffering only adds to my own.

The waves of devastation caused by Carty's and Brown's greed and bravado roll on and on. The attack which they carried out on Tom was barbaric. They showed him no mercy and have shown absolutely no remorse since.

They have made the experience even more agonising by refusing to face up to and admit to their crime and by dragging me, our families and friends through a full trial. Greed fuelled Carty's and Brown's attack on Tom but it is obvious, particularly from the trademark injury which they inflicted on his left leg, that they were also trying to play the 'big man'.

I despair at their deeply misguided sense of logic – because it is not a man who attacks a defenceless person with a knife, or any other weapon, or hunts victims down in a pack – it is a complete coward – someone who lacks the confidence to take someone on an equal footing and instead feels the need to put themselves at an unfair advantage.

There can be no sense of victory for Carty and Brown over Tom – he never stood a chance in the first place. He was alone, defenceless, and a stranger to violence.

I very much doubt that, as children, any of the hopes and aspirations they held for their future included killing a man and yet here they stand convicted of that heinous crime.

What happened along the way for them to become so cruel and hateful towards others and at such a young age?

What a huge waste of life – not just of Tom's but also of their own – years in prison for an Oyster card and a mobile telephone. How, on any level, could it have been worth it for them?

Tom did his best to make it home that night and he nearly made it. Although I was not there to help him, or to hold him in his final moments, as I desperately wish I had been, it comforts me to know that as he passed on from this world, he was absolutely safe and secure in the knowledge that it just would not be possible for me to love him any more than I do and will for ever.

There are no more tomorrows here for me and Tom and all of our hopes and dreams have been brutally torn away.

I just hope that there is something better for us on the other side. In the meantime, just as hate and bitterness had no place in Tom's life, neither will they in his memory.

I am determined to ensure, along with many others, that as much good as possible comes out of this horrific tragedy, so that I can say to Tom when I see him again, as I believe I will, 'That was the most agonising experience of my life, but everything that you worked so hard to achieve and everything of you that you left behind, was cherished and built upon to touch the lives of others in the way you would have wanted – and it was all done out of our great love for you.' My family, Tom's family and I are all so thankful that justice has been done for Tom.

We are enormously grateful to everyone involved in securing the convictions against Carty and Brown – for their relentless hard work, determination and support.

Even as these words were being spoken, Carty and Brown looked bored and yawned as if to show their indifference. The chasm between the worlds inhabited by the victim and his attackers seemed wider than ever.

It was examined by Tom's grieving father John who wrote a remarkable analysis of the events in *The Times*:

. . . My son's murder shows there is much work to be done. The judge said in his summing up that our son, Tom, 'was in the wrong place at just the wrong time'. That is one of the things that makes it so hard to accept his death. Had he left the tube station a little bit earlier, or a little bit later, he would still be with us. The possible 'ifs and buts' are endless. This is also what I feel when I start to consider what makes young men in Britain want to attack and kill innocent people like Tom.

Countless words have been written about his

murderers, *Donnel Carty* and *Delano Brown*, but I still cannot begin to understand their world. There the violence they used was so commonplace that just after they had killed Tom they strolled rather than ran off.

But unlike them, we cannot so easily ignore this scene of devastation. Understand we must, or at least we must try, if any good is to come of this. The first, and perhaps most obvious, point to note is that if the pair had not been carrying knives, not only would Tom have been spared, but their own lives would not have been ruined.

Next, there is a report from the Economic and Social Research Council, much quoted in connection with the verdict yesterday. Its authors found that 'street robbers often carry out their vicious attacks for kicks'. This seems to me to be a reflection of the world we live in, where violence is glorified in music, films and videos . . .

Also, there has been a rise in gang culture on our city streets. Here there are shades of West Side Story and that wonderful song 'Gee Officer Krupke', which puts the whole knotty problem in a nutshell: 'Gee, Officer Krupke, we're very upset' sing the gang members, 'We never had the love that ev'ry child oughta get./ We ain't no delinquents,/ We're misunderstood./ Deep down inside us there is good!'

Half a century later we are still, as in that musical, debating whether these gang members are 'crazy', 'lazy' *or 'sociologically sick'. What we do know is that they seem to want to celebrate their unique identity and independence from normal society. In London they use Jamaican patois and make up slang that only their friends can understand; they gain street cred. from wearing the latest designer clothes and having the most technically hot mobile phones; and they rap about their exploits. This is far from Broadway; this is* Clockwork Orange *come true.*

. . . Neither Brown nor Carty appear to have had a father around during their formative years, so the temptation to do what they liked, and to get rich quick without the bother of working must have been attractive if no one was around to teach them right from wrong. As was apparent at the trial, the concept of telling the truth, on oath, seemed to be completely alien to them . . .'

The impact of the death of a man loved by so many could be judged by the reaction of others who cared deeply for him.

His elder brother Mike wrote: 'Thomas would not have perceived these two youths to be a threat. They were small and the only threatening thing that he would have seen would have been the fact that they were there at all. He would not have been prepared for the level of violence that they were willing to use.'

He added, 'My brother was a unique individual and

extremely clever. He studied classical Greek and this learning had a profound interest for him. Going through his things, I still find little scraps of paper written in ancient Greek . . . My brother loved life and he loved music. He had a zest for life and he was very good at living.'

Mr ap Rhys Pryce told the London *Evening Standard* he had wondered whether his younger brother could have been saved. 'I now know that he could not, but I also have details of the manner of his death that will haunt me until I die. My brother died a horrible, violent death. He would have been scared and unprepared for the level of violence that was used against him. Tom's murder will haunt me for the rest of my life, knowing that he died alone in the road just yards from his home and the loving arms of his fiancée. I will miss my brother deeply and miss the future of growing old together that we would have had.'

Tom's mother Estella also spoke with the anguish of any mother, regardless of her background, about his death and its impact. She said 'I think about Tom every day and have many happy memories of him – bouncing out of nursery school to have a hug, learning to ride with his brother . . . He had a great enthusiasm and zest for life. Tom was the kind of son that any mother would want to have. The gentlest of people who would never willingly hurt anyone . . .

'Losing Tom so suddenly and in such a senseless way

has left a gap which can never truly be filled. I last saw Tom on Christmas Eve last year, as he spent Christmas Day, his first away from home, with his fiancée and her family. I would give anything to have him coming home for Christmas again, to see him on my doorstep giving me his all-embracing hug. Tom left us at the happiest time of his life, working in a job that was his vocation and making plans for his marriage in September this year to his beloved Adele. The impact of this event has been to make me think more about how crime can be prevented. When there are victims like Tom – and there seem to be many in the news now – prevention is obviously far better than cure.

So what of the young men convicted of Tom's murder, who appear to hold life so cheaply – the cost of a mobile phone and maybe some cash? I wonder if they have any understanding of how precious that life was to all Tom's family and friends and, of course, to his fiancée Adele? I have no wish for revenge and I hope that their lives can be reformed, and that they can learn to understand that greed, robbery and worst of all, murder, which is a truly terrible crime, cannot go unpunished, and that they have to take responsibility for their own actions.'

If only Brown and Carty had been raised in an environment of such care for others and awareness of society as a whole, rather than merely the narrow, hate-filled world devoid of any genuine aspiration they inhabited, then perhaps the tragedy would not have unfolded the way it did.

But their behaviour could not be viewed in isolation.

In March 2007 six other members of the KG Tribe were jailed indefinitely for their reign of terror which led to an estimated 150 attacks on innocent people.

The judge at Middlesex Guildhall Crown Court branded four of the defendants 'callous cowards and bullies' and said it was one of the worst robbery sprees of its kind he had ever heard of.

Toyan 'Flips' Vassall, eighteen, of Culver Grove, Stanmore, Ishmael Cowell, twenty-three, from Sandhurst Avenue, Harrow, Harry Bees, seventeen, of Parkthorne Drive, Harrow, and Kariem Al-Ebadi, eighteen, of Willesden Lane, Willesden, were all convicted of conspiracy to rob between 18 December 2005 and 15 January 2006 on an indictment limited to a sample thirty-six of the seventy or so tube attacks.

In addition, Vassall, Cowell and Bees were variously found guilty of three charges of wounding with intent. None showed any reaction as Judge Henry Blacksell, QC told them he regarded each as a 'high risk' to the public.

Indeterminate sentences for public protection were therefore inevitable and all of them would have to serve a minimum five years behind bars before being eligible for parole.

The judge had already dealt with two of the gang: Aaron 'Red Rat' Dennis, nineteen, the gang member who compiled the mugging guide, was jailed for at least five years after he admitted conspiracy to rob and a spate of wounding offences, and also jailed for a minimum of five years was Sebastian 'Icer' or 'Grove' Chidi, eighteen, who said, 'That's nothing, man,' after he was sent down by the judge.

Referring to their reign of terror, the judge said: 'This is a dreadful case. It is quite rightly, in my judgement, one which the general public are most concerned about, and they are the victims in this case.

'We are all, every travelling member of the public on the Underground in London, a victim as a result of what you were involved in and what you have been convicted of.

'This conspiracy involved you as a group over this period of time, showing no concern at all for the general public. Rather you preyed on the general public in a callous, cynical way. You abused and terrified the public in a way which is in itself totally unjustified.'

He continued: 'It has been described as being ruthless and well-organised ... I have absolutely no doubt that you as a group were particularly well practised in what you were doing. You worked together and were well-organised. The evidence demonstrates quite how ruthless you were.

'You are cowards, you are bullies, you taunt people, and you contrive situations so you had a pretext to assault people.

'The dreadful aspect of this case is how you left people traumatised because they couldn't actually intervene to help their fellow men. You left people having to live with themselves because they knew if they intervened they were likely to be stabbed, assaulted, a gun shown to them, left helpless ... you didn't care a jot. This case, in my judgement, must be one of the most serious of its kind. It is not just the taking of the property, outrageous though that is, but the fact you enjoyed humiliating people and beating them up.

'We have all seen CCTV images of people limping and bleeding, while you are jumping barriers, laughing,' he said.

Carty and Brown were sentenced to life imprisonment. Carty's sentence carried a minimum of twenty-one years behind bars and Brown had a seventeen-year tariff, although this was later increased to twenty by the Court of Appeal as the original term was 'unduly lenient'.

Yet the KG Tribe weren't the only ones infected with the disease of violence that surrounded Carty and Brown.

Carty's cousin Lloywen Carty, twenty-six, was part of another gang which shot Lee 'Mark' Subaran, twenty-seven, at a street party after the Notting Hill Carnival in 2004. The shots were fired despite 600 people being tightly packed on to an area outside Kensal Green station.

Both the Cartys were living with their grand-father in Burrows Road when Tom was murdered and both killings took place within a few streets of each other.

Lloywen Carty was found guilty of murder together with Conroy Smith, twenty-nine, a kitchen assistant of Harlesden, north London, and Jermaine Labastide, twenty-eight, a music promoter, of Kennington. They were all jailed for life with a minimum term of thirty years behind bars. Three other gang members – Leon Roberts, Tafari Dacas and Shane Taylor – were convicted and jailed for life, with the same minimum terms.

Old Bailey judge Stephen Kramer praised police for the difficult investigation into the Mus Luv Crew gang to which the accused belonged.

He said: 'Whatever the motive was for this cold-blooded execution, he did not deserve that death.'

In the aftermath of such events it is hard, almost clichéd, to say that 'good came out of evil' and yet that is what happened.

Tom's parents, his fiancée and Linklaters established a registered charity in the form of a trust as a lasting memorial to him. In his youth he had been a benefi-ciary of educational funding for which he was always grateful and one of the Trust's goals was, in their own words, to provide educational and vocational training opportunities to individuals who might not otherwise have access to them, in the hope that they too can achieve their potential and lead rewarding lives.

Poignantly it was also 'to help tackle the root causes of violent gang culture and violent street crime. In this way, the donations made to Tom's Trust are being used to ensure that as much good as possible comes out of Tom's tragic and senseless death.'

Eighteen months after that night of savagery in Kensal Green the Trust had raised over £1 million and among the many organisations to benefit were a refugee project at a primary school in Southall in west London and a boxing programme in Haringey in north London which combined sporting and academic tuition for youngsters in the area.

The Trust, in association with Tom's old school, Marlborough College, was also establishing the Tom ap Rhys Pryce Memorial Bursary, a means-tested bursary to be awarded once every five years to enable a child to attend the school.

Perhaps it is only fitting that the final words should be from Adele Eastman. In April 2008 she ran the London Marathon and raised over £25,000 for Tom's charity.

She wrote:

Nothing could have prepared me for the sense of loss and devastation which has followed. However, an extremely positive focus in my life is the charity which was set up in lasting memory of Tom soon after his death . . . We are determined to ensure that Tom's death has not been in vain, and that as much good as possible comes out of this horrific tragedy.

The objectives of Tom's Trust are to provide educational and vocational training opportunities for disadvantaged children and youths who might not otherwise have access to them, and to help tackle and prevent the root causes of violent gang culture and violent street crime.

Tom's Trust is already funding a number of worthwhile projects. However, with an increasing disparity in wealth and opportunity in this country, 27 youths murdered in London alone in 2007, and several more already this year, and with many of the organisations who are trying to tackle these problems struggling for funding, there is an acute and urgent need to provide more help.

I am running the marathon for Tom and also for the children and youths who benefit from his Trust – for whom, in many cases, it takes great strength and courage to face each day, as a result of living in poverty and/or suffering from abuse, neglect, or violence. Many are left feeling disaffected, angry and without any sense of hope.

Bitterness and anger could easily be excused, instead she concluded:

I believe we each have a responsibility to do whatever we can (no matter how great or small) to help those who are less fortunate than ourselves, and to tackle and overcome the escalating serious youth violence in this country. I very much hope that through Tom's Trust, we can encourage and support many children and youths to reach out for a better life for themselves.

11

Older and wiser men than Shakilus Townsend have fallen for the sweet, yet deceitful, words of a young woman, only later to bitterly regret their mistake. Shakilus was just sixteen when he became the victim of a 'honeytrap' and paid the highest possible price – his life.

He was so besotted with Samantha Joseph, an attractive girl a year younger than him, that he proudly told his mother he loved her and planned to marry the girl. But that infatuation was to lead him to a terrible fate in an alley in south London, the victim of a gang who stabbed and beat him to death.

The events that led to his murder had an almost melodramatic cast to them, albeit in a modern, violent setting: two young men both infatuated with a girl who moves from one to another with ease and finally makes her choice with deadly consequences for the jilted suitor. It is a story as old as the hills, but no less tragic because of its almost clichéd circumstances.

Shakilus died because he was caught in the love triangle involving himself, Joseph and an eighteen-year-old called Danny 'Tamper' McLean who was a member of the SMN – 'Shine My Nine' – gang in Croydon, so named after an obscene reference to a sex act, and whose members wore bright orange bandannas to signify their membership. For almost a month, unknown to McLean, Joseph had been seeing Shakilus after first meeting him on a bus, and the boy had subsequently showered her with gifts. McLean discovered her duplicity, but the capricious Joseph then decided she wanted to return to him and would do anything she could to achieve that – even if it was to end in violence and tragedy for Shakilus.

When he found out that he had been two timed McLean was furious even though Joseph was determined – despite being subjected to frequent beatings by McLean – to get her old boyfriend back. There was one certain way that she could do that – she could 'deliver' poor Shakilus to him. So Joseph hatched a plan in which she said she would introduce Shakilus to a cousin of hers, and to that end on a Thursday afternoon in July 2008, she met up with the youngster.

Perhaps it shouldn't be too surprising, given the surveillance age in which we live in, but the moment the trap was sprung was actually recorded on camera.

It was on a bus and the vehicle's CCTV camera captured the two of them standing alongside each other. When Shakilus wasn't looking, Joseph, wearing a see-through floral dress, sent a text message on her mobile phone. It wasn't the idle, innocuous chatter of most teenagers. This message was confirmation that the victim was about to be delivered to Tamper and five other masked and hooded gang members who were to end his life.

Shakilus said at one stage, 'I hope you and your cousin aren't getting me set,' and she replied: 'Do you really think I'd do that?' He was soon to have the answer.

The gang set on him when he arrived for the meeting-that-wasn't in Beulah Crescent, Thornton Heath, and one of them, sixteen-year-old Andre Thompson, beat him with a baseball bat while others kicked and stabbed him. When it came to McLean's turn to stab the victim he twisted the knife inside his body in a perverted act of vengeance that left a gaping hole in his stomach, one of the six stab wounds in his young body.

Neighbours ran to the scene and found the doomed boy crying: 'Mummy, Mummy, Mummy . . . I don't want to die.'

Local resident Dee Bamima witnessed the brutal attack from her window and rushed to help stricken Shakilus. Dee, thirty-five, said: 'He kept saying, "I don't want to die, I don't want to die" and was screaming for his mum, asking where she was. One of the neighbours had brought a towel and we put it round his chest to try to stop the bleeding. I touched him and spoke to him. I asked him his name. He was talking really well. I asked if he knew the boys who attacked him and he said no. He was asking for his mum. I asked him what his mum's name was and her phone number. He didn't have his mum's number because he didn't have his mobile. He was trying to get up but he couldn't. He was bleeding a lot. It was about ten or twenty minutes that I was with him. We tried to get him to calm down and to lie down and lie on his side as he was gasping for air. He was very shocked, his eyes were very wide and he looked very afraid. He was very scared and his last words were "I can't breathe."'

She added: 'I heard the gang shouting, "Get him from the other side" so they had obviously planned it all. They had scarves over their faces and beat him using a baseball bat, before stabbing him in the chest.'

Richard Higgins, who lived in the block of flats near where Shakilus was killed, said: 'I thought he had fallen over some workman's tools but then I saw the amount of blood. I spotted an eight-inch kitchen knife that had been used. He had been stabbed in the stomach and it looked like his chest had been cut open.'

Housewife Sharon Simpson, forty-seven, said she saw the killers laying into their victim on a lawn just eighteen feet from her front-room window. She opened the window and screamed: "Leave him alone!" and ran out of her flat to confront them. 'I saw this little boy running for his life with three men in masks chasing him. They had bandannas tied over their faces. They tackled the boy and got him on the ground and they were just hitting him again and again. They were murdering him and wouldn't stop. When I screamed, "Leave him alone!" again one of them looked me in the eyes and said, "We know who you are." But I just kept screaming and they ran.'

After the 2 p.m. attack, another CCTV camera minutes later captured Joseph walking beside McLean, carrying his hooded top and a cream-coloured handbag stained with blood. She later confessed to friends that she had agreed to 'get Shak set' and only liked him because he lavished her with gifts.

McLean wasn't the only one of the gang to have a frightening 'pedigree'. Alongside him were Tyrell Ellis, nineteen, and his brother Don-Carlos Ellis, eighteen, for whom the killing was an act to help them on their way to fulfil their dreams of being gangsters.

Tyrell, known as 'Drastik', was subject to a two-year ASBO for gang-related crimes, while Don-Carlos, called 'Rugz', was on bail and due to report to a police station on the day of the killing. Others in the deadly group were Andre Johnson-Haynes, eighteen, a former public-school boy from Croydon who played rugby for London Irish, and Michael Akinfenwa, seventeen.

Word of the slaying and Joseph's betrayal soon

spread, and Shakilus's friends quickly used social networking sites to name and shame her. One comment read: 'Remember u set up Shak. You bitch. And he luved yooooh. You iz f****d!'

Joseph had even been told by friends before that day of death that she should not let boys fight over her, only to reply with simple street logic, 'Either I get the beats or he gets the beats. Tamper wants to get Shak set.'

Tragic as Shakilus's death was, it wasn't long before another aspect of his life emerged.

Pictures of him were posted on the internet showing him wielding a knife and posing with a gun. There were strong suggestions of gang connections as Shakilus, who had convictions for weapons' offences and assault, was described as a 'fallen soldier' and there were vows to avenge his killing.

But soon after the slaying arrests were made and, a year later, the murder trial began of Joseph and the other gang members where the honeytrap that led to Shakilus's death was described to an Old Bailey jury.

Brian Altman, QC, prosecuting, said: 'Shakilus had been seeing her [Joseph] for a matter of weeks, but she was playing a dangerous game, because she was cheating on Danny McLean. It is clear that he had come to learn of her deception and, by way of recompense, she agreed to set up the hapless Shakilus Townsend in a honey-trap with a lethal and tragic twist. She was more than equal to the task. She played her part to perfection, duping Shakilus who could see no wrong in her, the others in hot pursuit of him.'

He added: 'Despite their ages, this attack was pre-arranged and pre-planned, and it was executed meticulously, and with consummate skill and cunning.'

A day after the killing the victim's account on the social networking site Bebo was cancelled from a laptop found at McLean's address – Shakilus's username, e-mail address and password had been entered on the computer to do so, the prosecutor said. Mr Altman added: 'It is reasonable to conclude that it was Joseph who was accessing the account, with details she had from him. What she did was to cancel Shakilus's account, doubtless an attempt to rub out any other evidence of her relationship and connection with him.'

Joseph admitted in court to leading Shakilus to the ambush, but claimed she did not realise he would get seriously hurt, saying: 'I understand "set" to mean have a fight, beating him up.'

Asked if she wanted him stabbed or thought he might be stabbed, she replied 'no' although she admitted she told Shakilus they were going to see a friend only for him to be chased by McLean and other youths near some garages.

After she walked away, McLean caught up with her and she knew something had gone wrong because his head was bleeding, she claimed. 'I didn't know what was going on. That was not what I expected to happen.'

McLean admitted he routinely carried a knife, he claimed he needed it to protect himself and his family, and that he acted in self-defence against Shakilus. Nevertheless, after a lengthy trial and long deliberation by the jury, the seven-strong group were found guilty of murder, with sentencing to be later, leaving behind, as always, grieving relatives for the victim of crime.

Shakilus's father Derek, a 45-year-old HGV driver, said after the killing he had been unaware of his son's links with teen gangs: 'I was devastated, shocked, horrified and amazed. I didn't know what he was doing when he was out of sight. He was a kid. Around us he behaved like a kid. We had no idea. The Shakilus we knew organised a surprise birthday party for his mum.'

He added: 'My message to youngsters is, "Leave knives alone." If you are walking on the street with one, you have only one intention.'

And the youngster's mother Nicola, thirty-three, from Deptford, south-east London, felt a mother's grief: 'My son wasn't perfect. But he was a vibrant, loving boy.

'He said he was really in love with this girl, that she was to be his future wife and that she was going to have his kids – he was really smitten with her. I've never met her but I have spoken to her on the phone. Shaki showed me pictures on his mobile phone and I remember thinking she really is pretty. He was popular and always had girlfriends, but the girl on trial was different. He really cared about her and I can't understand how she could have callously set him up and lured him to his death. Shakilus's death was a senseless premeditated murder and nobody deserves to die in the appalling way my son did, especially not a child.'

She also pleaded with teenage gangs to put down their weapons, saying: 'You may think you're in too deep, but you can change. Don't wait until tomorrow. Tomorrow may be too late.'

The seven all eventually received life sentences and, passing sentence, Judge Richard Hawkins said Joseph had fallen 'under the malign influence' of McLean in a callous attack. He told the group: 'You left him to die a lonely death, crying for his mother.' Joseph was ordered to be detained for a minimum of ten years and the evil McLean was sentenced to a minimum of fifteen years. Thompson was ordered to serve at least fourteen years before being eligible for parole and the other four were told they must serve at least twelve years.

After the gang was sentenced Shakilus's mother added: 'My feelings about Shaki's death are a mixture of ever-changing emotions that neither words nor tears can explain. I have been robbed of a very rare and precious gem. He was loved, cherished and needed. The manner in which he died tarnishes every loving memory that we hold of him, because, when we think of his life, we are inevitably left with heartbreaking thoughts and feelings of its tragic end. I am unable to understand why these youngsters felt that they needed to use the brutality they did, which, in turn, resulted in my son's life coming to a tragic and abrupt end.

'I see them in the dock, laughing amongst themselves, and I am once again consumed with anger. To think that they ended the life of a living, breathing human being and they have shown no genuine remorse. Every day we sit and look at these seven accused, in my eyes, children. They were meant to have been focused on school or college, enjoying what should have been a bright future.

'Shaki was sixteen with his whole life ahead of him, finally ready to put childhood wrong-doings behind him and live up to his potential of becoming the great young man I know he could have been. The reality that these young people with no souls had such a disregard for life that they deliberately conspired to use manipulation to cause nothing short of destruction is absolutely soul-destroying for me.'

12

David Idowu was due to give a speech urging young people to give up knives. He never made it. Instead, on 17 June 2008, a few days before his scheduled appearance in a public speaking contest, David became one of the youngest victims of knife crime in Britain. He was just fourteen years old.

It was at 5 p.m. on that mid-June day that David had closed the front door of his house on the Tabard estate in Southwark, south-east London, and walked across the road into Talbot Gardens, the park opposite, to play football with his friends. Less than an hour later two police officers walked into the Tesco where his mother Grace worked and walked towards her till. At first she thought there must have been a shoplifting offence in the store, but they asked her to go with them into the supermarket's office and there they told her that her son had been stabbed.

Two weeks earlier she had watched a television report

on the stabbing to death of a fifteen-year-old girl, Arsema Dawit, on an estate in nearby Waterloo, central London.

'I just saw it and thought it was very sad that this young girl should die like this. I never imagined as I watched, that my son would be next.'

The police told her that David had been attacked near their home. 'It was like the life was suddenly sucked out of me. I collapsed and I came round to hear them shouting my name. They drove me to the Royal London Hospital where they were operating on David. They had resuscitated him twice before they started the surgery. The knife had been thrust deep into his chest and pierced his heart. David lost 90 per cent of his blood, they fought so hard to save him.'

The operation to try to save David's life lasted five hours. Afterwards Grace's husband Tim and their other children were allowed to see David in the intensive care unit where he lay wired to machines and unconscious.

For almost three weeks she sat at her son's bedside holding his hand and stroking his forehead.

'When I called his name he would turn his head to me. His eyes were wide open but he could not see me, he just turned his head towards the sound. The doctors told me he may not survive but I was determined he would, then they told me he would be brain-damaged but I wanted him back no matter what state he was in.'

'All he had done was go across the park to play football with his brother. That's all children want to be able to do, to go to the park, to go around the corner to buy sweets, to go into a shop and buy some trainers. Why is it that they can't do that safely any more?'

Two weeks after he was stabbed a photograph was taken of David: his face was swollen, his eyes closed and a tube protruded from his mouth. He had to have a feeding drip to keep him hydrated and a heart monitor was constantly measuring his condition. Five days later he died. Grace was to later take the remarkable decision to publicly release the haunting image.

'That is my beautiful boy. I want this picture published so people can see what happened to him. I want young people to see what happens when you put a knife in someone. They should just stop all this. He was not a criminal, he was an innocent boy. All this is for nothing.'

David was the nineteenth teenager to die in London in 2008 after being stabbed. In the brief period between his attack and his death seven more teenagers had been fatally stabbed or shot dead, meaning teenage homicides in the first nine months of that year had already matched the number for all of 2007 in the Metropolitan Police area.

David Idowu was already good at graphics and designed backgrounds for MySpace pages and was talking of going to university. Although he may have been a model student and son, the same could not be said of Elijah Dayoni, the sixteen-year-old who took his life, who, only one day before the stabbing, had been given a supervision order for burglary.

Congo-born Dayoni was raised by his grandmother in Angola before joining his parents in Britain in 2000, but in his short time in this country he had a string of convictions and in the previous two years had mugged a man, been excluded from school for carrying a replica gun and carried out a burglary. The supervision order was imposed for an earlier offence of shoplifting.

He attacked without warning or reason and stabbed David in the heart. As David attempted to escape, Dayoni chased him, and a CCTV image showed the attacker smiling and laughing as he did so.

David collapsed on the street where passers-by helped to keep his heart going, but it stopped twice. When he was arrested two days later Dayoni, who had been called to the park by his younger brothers after a conflict between boys from their school and Walworth Academy where David was a pupil, was still wearing a T-shirt with the younger boy's blood on it.

Days after David's death his bus-driver father Tim said, 'He always thought of what to do now and what will happen in the future. He believed change can only come through good world leaders and had recently visited Madame Tussaud's to have his picture taken with President Clinton, who he admired and wanted to emulate . . . Our lives can never be the same again.'

Grace, forty-eight, knelt down at the spot where

David died to lead a tearful rendition of 'Amazing Grace' with friends and family. She said: 'We love you, David, but God loves you more. May your heart and soul rest in peace. I know my redeemer lives.

'David gave his life to Jesus Christ when he was ten years old. The thief does not come except to steal and kill and to destroy, but Jesus Christ came that we may have life and have it more abundantly. David is with his Heavenly Father but we shall see him again. The body of Christ – let us call for revival on this great nation and God will hear us.'

Pastor Emmanuel Medaiyese, of the Christ Apostolic Church in south Bermondsey, said: 'David was a very complete, very gentle boy. He was never involved in any gangs or anything like that. He was more interested in working hard at school and studying. David was a lovely boy who loved playing football. He was very active at church and was in our youth group. David didn't deserve this.'

At the end of July a slow march to Downing Street took place to try to end the epidemic of knife attacks in the area where David's life was cut short.

The protest started at the junction of Great Dover Street and Becket Street in Borough. David's family, friends, fellow churchgoers, pastors, politicians and complete strangers then set off on the rally to Downing Street behind Mr and Mrs Idowu.

Grace told the marchers: 'Knife crime should be addressed by everyone; everybody in this society. Whose life is to be taken next? Demons are possessing these younger ones to carry knives in order to destroy what we hold precious.'

Southwark and Bermondsey MP Simon Hughes also addressed the crowd before embracing David's parents. Wearing a T-shirt emblazoned with the teenager's face, he said: 'It isn't inevitable that children stab each other with knives. It doesn't have to be like that.'

David's grieving parents met Prime Minister Gordon Brown and were invited into Number 10 after leading hundreds on the march. In a meeting with Mr Brown they presented their manifesto for change, calling for tougher sentences for knife criminals.

Grace said: 'We discussed what we believe will help us end knife crime. We asked for a new national holiday for people of all faiths to pray together. And we want being caught with a knife to be a strict liability offence with tougher sentences for offenders. Life should mean life. My son Peter also asked Mr Brown for more money to be put into provision for youth activities. Mr Brown promised us he will look at our petition and take action. We trust him and his promise.'

In their letter delivered to Number 10 David's grieving parents said:

We the family and friends of David Idowu believe knife crime is the most worrying high-profile issue in London. Without urgent action with solutions to the causes, we believe the government is condemning children, particularly in the black communities, to a life of fear – and in some cases death. No child should fear that his or her school uniform will condemn them to death as they walk to or from school. No child should fear another child because they have left one neighbourhood and entered another. No child should have to face a knife in the way David did.

David's eighteen-year-old brother Peter also met the Prime Minister and asked him why his brother had to die.

'I was brought up to know if you speak the truth there is nothing to fear. My fourteen-year-old brother died only three miles from Downing Street, and I wanted Mr Brown to tell me why he got stabbed. He was not involved in any quarrels. He was not involved in any gang, so how could this happen to him? What did he do to deserve this?

'David was the one who lit up the house and made everybody laugh. Without him our home is so quiet. My little brother was very close to David and he has taken it very hard. He is trying to be strong for everyone, but he is only thirteen.

'The Prime Minister listened to me. He said I had

some very good ideas. What's important now is that things change. He said he will tackle this problem of knives and guns, and I hope he will. David had written a speech about knives and guns on our streets that he was due to deliver at a school debating contest just before he died. 'David wanted it to have a good chance at the competition, so he gave it to my dad to read to check it over. My dad said it was so good he was going to take a day off work to see him deliver the speech.'

Peter, David and youngest brother James grew up in nearby Peckham before moving to the Tabard estate three years earlier. 'I never thought to be afraid walking the streets around here. But since David was stabbed, I feel differently. Sometimes I look at groups of boys hanging around on the street and feel intimidated,' Peter said.

'The day of the stabbing was just a normal school day when David and my brother James got up to go to school. Later that day I came back from college and got a call from my mother saying my brother had been stabbed and was in hospital. At first I didn't know what to think, I found it very hard to believe and thoughts plagued my mind ... why would my brother get stabbed? Three weeks later, when I got the news that my little brother was no more, I broke down.

'What is this country coming to when we believe it is fashionable to carry a knife and use it? If this continues the next generation will be wiped out. The important thing is to know this is something that is affecting all communities. Black, white, poor, rich . . . everyone needs to come together to fight this.'

A month after the Downing Street march James and Peter were joined by 400 other relatives and mourners for David's funeral when they gathered at the spot where he was found stabbed. A small white coffin was drawn a quarter of a mile by two white horses pulling a white carriage to St George the Martyr Church in Borough. On the carriage were wreaths that read 'Son', 'Brother' and 'Cousin'. At the private service, conducted by the Revd Ray Andrews, a letter was read aloud from David's friend Paige, who had known him since nursery school and was a fellow pupil at Walworth Academy.

It said:

Now I've only just realised how short life really is and it's disgraceful how innocent young people like you and many others get killed for no reason. I miss you so much and now you are gone life won't be the same without you.

Dayoni was eventually found guilty of murder at the Old Bailey and was ordered to be detained during Her Majesty's Pleasure, serving a minimum of twelve years.

David's parents watched from the public gallery as Mrs Idowu's moving impact statement was read to the court by prosecution counsel David Waters, QC.

Mrs Idowu said she had said goodbye to her son that

morning as he went to school and she went to work, not realising it was the last time they would talk to each other. She said: 'He left for school saying "See you Mummy." Nothing told me that would be the end of seeing my son alive.' And she described how she, her husband and sons watched helplessly as David suffered after being knifed in the heart. 'Our dream child lost his struggle to live,' she said.

She described her son as 'a handsome, athletic fourteen-year-old' who was doing well at school and wanted to be an aeronautics engineer. 'We will never recover from the loss and from witnessing the pain he endured. The knife which pierced David's heart will keep the wounds open in our hearts for ever.'

There was also one terrible coincidence in the tragic death of David. Ben Kinsella, the brother of *EastEnders* actress Brooke Kinsella, had spoken the previous year in the same contest – Jack Petchey's Speak Out challenge – that David was due to appear in.

Less than two weeks after David was stabbed and while he lay in his hospital bed losing his fight for life, Ben, sixteen, was knifed too, eleven times, on a north London street at 2 a.m. He, like David, was to be added to the ever-increasing list of teenagers who lost their knives to the thrust of a blade.

13

Facebook is a phenomenon of the internet age.

It was born in 2004 in the room of nineteen-year-old Harvard University second-year computer science and psychology student Mark Zuckerberg and his pals who took just a week to work out the program for the site.

In no time at all the social networking website was enabling people to exchange news, gossip and information. Most of it is harmless, a lot of it informative and stimulating. Soon Facebook had left behind the American colleges and universities it was born in, and millions were using it every day as it conquered the world. It was to make Zuckerberg and his friends a fortune.

When it was just a few weeks old and already catching on like wildfire, he explained one of the reasons he had created it: 'I know it sounds corny, but I'd love to improve people's lives, especially socially.'

Bolton, to the north-west of Manchester, is a former

mill town probably now best known as being the inspirational hometown of comic Peter Kay with his irre-
pressible local humour. It's a long way, in every sense,
from the cerebral, sedate campuses of Ivy League America.

And when Facebook and Bolton were linked in the
public mind it was not because of an act 'to improve
people's lives'. Far from it.

On the night of 12 July 2008, Leon Ramsden posted
a message on his own Facebook site telling everyone:
'i feel like killin some1 need to stay of the hard stuff
ha f*** it it's Saturday ha.' Within a few hours he was
to prove as good as his twisted word: Paul Gilligan, a
31-year-old father of three, was dead after being stabbed
in a pub in the centre of the town, an area filled with
bars and fast-food outlets. It was a terrible, needless loss
of life in any circumstance. It would have been tragic
if it were isolated, but he was yet another victim of a
spate of knife crimes that was inexorably rising out of
control.

Across the nation there were knifings galore and
Bolton was a microcosm of that disease: a small town
with a population of only 130,000, yet there were five
knifings – two of them in one incident – in the brutal
forty-eight-hour period that saw Mr Gilligan's life come
to an end. There were an incredible 114 incidents
involving knives in 'friendly' Bolton in just one year.

It would be repetitive to catalogue every other knife

crime outside Bolton during the epidemic of stabbings before Mr Gilligan's death, but to illustrate the continuing growth of the problem, here is a snapshot of a nation on the brink in the days before his death. It is important to remember that these are just some of the knife crimes that attracted media attention; others would not have rated a mention in the press or were not reported to the authorities in the first place:

July 3 – Shakilus Townsend, 16, died 4 July after being lured into an ambush by his girlfriend Samantha Joseph.

July 7 – Schoolboy David Idowu, fourteen, died almost three weeks after being stabbed in an attack in Great Dover Street, Southwark, London.

July 7 – Dylan Fox, twenty-one, stabbed to death in Durrants Road, Bethnal Green, east London.

July 8 – 43-year-old man, fatally stabbed at a house in Hazel Grove, Crewe.

July 9 – 25-year-old Mark Beard stabbed to death outside a house in Caldon Green, Bulwell, Nottingham.

July 10 – 45-year-old Joanne De Asha found stabbed to death in a home in Crosby, Liverpool.

July 10 – 41-year-old Latvian Gennar Jaronis found dead after suffering head injuries and slash wounds at the rear of a disused pub in Tottenham High Road, London.

July 10 – eighteen-year-old Melvin Bryan was fatally stabbed in an attack at a bedsit in Gloucester Road, Edmonton, north London.

July 10 – Adnan Patel, twenty, was fatally injured in Downsell Road, Leyton, east London. He had been stabbed in a confrontation with a gang of men and crashed his black Ford focus as he tried to escape.

July 10 – Yusufu Miiro, twenty, died after he was stabbed in the head and chest in St David's Court, Walthamstow, north-east London.

July 11 – twenty-year-old Thomas Coombs Duffield died after a stabbing in west Bromwich, following a row in the street on the evening of 10 July.

July 13 – father-of-two died after being stabbed following a row in Withywood, Bristol, on the evening of 12 July.

A glimpse of Britain in the midst of knife crime – and those were only the cases that attracted national publicity.

The week ended with Paul Gilligan losing his life in the Pepper Alley pub in Bolton town centre.

Peter Fahy, who was soon afterwards to become Chief Constable of Greater Manchester, later commented on the crisis: 'I am concerned that we seem to be producing a lot of angry young men at the moment. We need to understand why that is and why some of these young men are quite prepared to use extremes of violence over nothing. We are continuing to work to try and reduce that level of aggression in town centres with pubs, clubs and restaurants.'

Mr Fahy said initiatives, including the use of knife arches similar to metal detectors in airports, had helped, but the continued availability of cheap alcohol was something that could not be ignored: 'The fact that you can now buy alcohol from every late night shop and petrol station and that it's so much cheaper must have an impact,' he told the local newspaper, the *Bolton Evening News*. 'I think alcohol plays a part, but we are also concerned about the mixture of alcohol and cocaine.'

He wasn't the only senior policeman to be concerned about the situation. Deputy Assistant Commissioner Alf Hitchcock of the Metropolitan Police had been chosen by Home Secretary Jacqui Smith to help combat knife crime in eight hotspot areas of the country. He was, inevitably, dubbed 'Britain's Knife Czar' as a result.

Mr Hitchcock's brief was to focus on the knife crime problem areas of London, the West Midlands, Greater Manchester, Merseyside, Lancashire, Essex, Thames Valley and West Yorkshire. The first wave of forces would develop common practices on intelligence gathering, stop-and-search, enforcement, prosecution and educating young people about how to stay safe. Other forces would then be required to adopt the same tactics.

Mr Hitchcock was, of course, under no illusion about

the task ahead of him.

He made it clear that effective policing could reduce knife attacks in the short term but would not provide a long-term solution. He admitted it was 'hugely worrying' that the annual number of hospital admissions for knife injuries had risen in recent years from 3,000 to 5,000 while the age of those carrying and using knives had fallen steeply.

Speaking on his first day in the job, the day after Paul Gilligan died, he also suggested jobless teenagers should be sent on a form of 'national service' – a non-military programme could include helping vulnerable people and overseas aid work. Tellingly he said that a far-reaching, twenty-year national plan to deal with children and young adults was needed.

'Most kids are not beyond the pale. Most kids are decent young people. We have let them down. Now it's time to give them the hope they deserve.'

Many of his 'national service' personnel would be teenagers who had dropped out of school and might otherwise be drawn to crime as a career and gangs as a surrogate family. 'It should be something where they can learn skills and help people. It would give them a sense of responsibility and achievement – and some discipline. It should not be seen as a punishment, or a pressurised duty like conscription, but as an opportunity to go forward into a successful adulthood.'

Offenders and their victims, once typically in their

late teens or early twenties, were more likely to be in their mid or even early teens now, and police were seeing an 'intensification in the severity' of attacks, he said.

'We've seen the problem of violence among young people getting worse. But it's not just knife crime. Knife crime is just symptomatic of larger issues. Of course we in the police are doing what we can to crack down – but policing cannot be the whole answer. After all, if we were able to stop and search every youngster estimated to be carrying a knife today, and they were all to be sent to prison, we'd be talking of tens of thousands. Around 90 per cent of youngsters – who do not carry knives – are decent kids but we have a duty to them to create a safe environment.

'The problem is not just the carrying of knives but the willingness to use them. Reports of incidents from hospitals show actual injuries have gone up from 3,000 a year to 5,500 a year. Parents are right to be concerned about the safety of their kids. And young people – especially in areas where knife-carrying may be more prevalent – are also right to be concerned. We need a comprehensive plan, starting with young children and their parents, giving them support and parenting skills. This kind of plan is not cheap and easy. Changes in government often mean changes in plans, so it needs cross-party support for a programme which may take fifteen to twenty years to achieve its full effect,' added Mr Hitchcock, who was also the spokesman on knife crime for the Association of Chief Police Officers.

The growing knife menace was not just a social or criminal problem though, it was also a political one. And the major parties were disagreeing over the measures needed to combat it, disagreements that led Mr Hitchcock to say: 'One of the worries I have is the way that this issue is being used politically at the moment. This is a time for the parties to stop using it as a political argument and to start working together. I'm sure there are good ideas in government and good ideas in the Opposition and drawing these ideas together would be better than fighting over the issue. We all know that policing alone isn't going to solve this. There is a far broader and deeper piece of work that needs to be done about how we plan over the next ten or fifteen or twenty years to solve these problems.'

Mr Hitchcock's observations about the unity needed to cope with the crime wave was appropriate. A storm was brewing over the head of the Home Secretary about one of the measures her department announced to confront the attacks. Plans for those who used knives in attacks to visit their victims in hospital were immediately roundly condemned.

Ms Smith said the hospital visits would make people realise that there was nothing glamorous about carrying a knife. 'I just think that's a better way of making people face up to the consequences of [their] action and making them more likely not to carry knives again in the future. The important message that we need to get over to young people is if you think you are safer going out on the streets carrying a knife you are wrong. You are likely to have that knife used against you, you could potentially end up using it against somebody else, your life will be ruined and the lives of others will be ruined as well.'

Ms Smith said that calling for all offenders to go to jail was 'simplistic'. But Dominic Grieve, the Shadow Home Secretary, said that her proposals were 'ill-thought-through, piecemeal announcements and failed initiatives', and demanded more jail terms for knife offenders. 'Sending serious offenders to visit victims in hospital is not anywhere near the same as sending them to prison. Not only would we have tough policing to tackle knife crime on our streets now, but under our plans people convicted of knife crime would automatically face the presumption of jail. This would act as a deterrent and punishment that is not only tough and effective, but also desperately needed.'

Chris Huhne, the Liberal Democrat home affairs spokesman, said American research had found that showing teenagers the consequences of other people's crimes did not work: 'Jacqui Smith is coming up with half-baked ideas because the government has been in denial about the scale of the knife crime problem.'

The idea was condemned by surgeons, patients' groups, MPs and crime experts too. The Royal College of Surgeons said the plan was 'distasteful' and 'morally, ethically and legally suspect'. Former trauma surgeon Jim Ryan, an emeritus professor at University College London, described it as a 'knee-jerk reaction of questionable value'.

He said: 'Notwithstanding the issue of consent, I can't imagine someone who has just been stabbed would want a knife offender watching their treatment. I also don't think staff who are having to deal with a stab victim in a fraught, high-intensity A&E ward would take kindly to some criminal watching what they were doing and getting in the way.'

Despite seemingly admitting to the scheme in a television interview, Ms Smith quickly backtracked on the idea of attackers meeting their victims in hospital. She said that the media had misunderstood the proposals, which were simply that at some stage knifemen would go to hospitals to see what damage they cause and on other occasions meet their victims. The two ideas had somehow been merged into one by the press, she said. Predictably it led to ridicule and cries of 'U-turn' from her critics and, in spite of her protests, the publicity that this 'measure that wasn't' attracted dominated the headlines.

On 14 July the government's widely trailed Youth Crime Action Plan was officially unveiled, and in it was a proposal that ministers would ask judges to consider widening the number of cases in which sixteen- and seventeen-year-old offenders could be publicly named, unlike the existing system where newspapers and broadcasters were banned from identifying criminals under eighteen, apart from in exceptional cases, usually involving extreme violence. If implemented, the new idea would mean anonymity being lifted far more regularly. Yet again the government came in for criticism.

Elizabeth Lovell of the Children's Society said: 'We are very concerned that it is in contravention of the UN Convention on the Rights of the Child which states that children under eighteen in trouble with the law will have a right to privacy. It could also become a badge of honour. The move could also hinder rehabilitation and integration into society.'

There was no evidence that identifying child criminals helped prevent crime, she added.

Harry Fletcher, assistant general secretary of probation union NAPO, said: 'These kids are already alienated by authority and this will just push them further away.'

The £100 million package from the government featured two schemes allowing young criminals to avoid being prosecuted for their actions if they took steps to improve their behaviour. The government said the new Youth Conditional Caution would be piloted the following year to 'reduce the number of young people being taken to court for relatively low-level offences while providing a robust response to their offending'. Ministers would also consider expanding a scheme in which children involved in low-level crime avoided prosecution if they met their victim and apologised. Eight police forces had been involved in a pilot version of the scheme, known as the Youth Restorative Disposal.

The document also proposed:

- Making more child criminals carry out 'reparation' such as unpaid work in the community on Friday and Saturday nights;
- Opening youth centres late in evenings and at weekends to keep youngsters occupied;
- Creating citizens' panels to give residents a say in the work young criminals should be forced to carry out in the community with them;
- Increasing the number of Asbos which also feature a parenting order, so the families have to become involved in improving a child's behaviour;
- Expanding a scheme which sees police remove lone children from the streets at night;
- Increasing police after-school patrols, targeting trouble-spots;
- Targeting the families of up to 20,000 unruly children by 2010 with a programme designed to improve behaviour, with the possibility of eviction from council houses if they failed to comply;

- Asking employers to improve employability of young people with criminal records, and ensuring suitable accommodation is available for young offenders when they leave custody.

Home Secretary Smith said: 'Increasingly we are able to identify these young people early and intervene to address the root causes of their behaviour, including supporting and challenging their parents in meeting their responsibilities. But I want to call on parents to play their part. Tough enforcement and policing is only one part of the solution.'

Justice Secretary Jack Straw said: 'For that small minority of out-of-control young people custody is the answer. The crimes they have committed are so serious that there can be no other way of dealing with them. If they deserve to be inside, they will go there. One aim of the new action plan is to divert young people away from crime, so that they are not unnecessarily drawn into the criminal justice system. The plan will ensure that those at risk of offending are identified as quickly as possible and, along with their families, are given appropriate levels of support to tackle the cause of their behaviour.'

A government survey published on the same day revealed nearly a third of primary-school-age children admit taking part in anti-social behaviour or other problem antics. The Home Office survey of nearly 6,000 youngsters aged between eight and ten found 30 per cent reported problem behaviour such as carrying a weapon, theft, arson, smoking and drinking alcohol.

Dominic Grieve was again not happy. 'Despite a decade of endless initiatives and a dedicated "respect agenda", anti-social behaviour is not only rising, but is being committed by younger and younger children. We need action at every level to fix our broken society – the government's failed policies are betraying a generation of young people.'

Prime Minister Gordon Brown weighed in too to the debate when he warned parents they had a duty to keep their children under control amid escalating public fears about youth knife crime. He said up to 20,000 families might face eviction from their homes if they failed to control their children.

These 20,000 were among a staggering 110,000 homes in which children were thought to be at risk of becoming prolific offenders – and where authorities were set to target special support. Knife-carrying youngsters were also threatened with being forced to spend their Friday and Saturday nights carrying out those hundreds of hours of community punishment.

After the series of high-profile stabbings which had thrust knife crime to the top of the political agenda, Mr Brown acknowledged at his regular Downing Street press conference that a great number of people felt insecure.

'Too many people, young and old, do not feel safe in the streets, and sometimes even in their homes, as a result of the behaviour of a minority. We need to make it absolutely clear to everyone, but especially young people, that in our country there are boundaries of acceptable behaviour [and] that it is completely unacceptable to carry a knife.' He said that youngsters carrying knives were more likely than ever to be caught, prosecuted and 'severely' punished, and he continually emphasised that responsibility lay with their parents.

'I think all of us recognise that the first responsibility where a child is in trouble or in danger of getting into trouble rests with the parent,' he said. Foreshadowing the £100 million plan being published the next day, Mr Brown said community punishments would be strengthened to make them 'tough, visible and effective'.

Mr Brown also declared that he disagreed with recent proposals from the Sentencing Guidelines Council – the body responsible, as its name indicates, for developing sentencing guidelines – to continue the practice of giving cautions and fines to those carrying knives. 'What the Sentencing Guidelines Council have said is not acceptable to me. What I want to see is anybody who is using a knife goes to prison; anybody who is carrying a knife is subject to either prison or a strong community payback that forces them to give service to the community,' he said. But he also stressed that jail or young offenders' institutions were not always the right approach, citing the example of a fourteen-year-old caught with a knife for the first time.

'What we should do is say to them, "There is a presumption to prosecute you will be punished." We are absolutely clear that that punishment will be severe. That punishment will include going to prison or tough community payback.'

The Prime Minister said there were more stop-and-searches being carried out than ever, more cash for such procedures and new presumption to prosecute offenders also meant they were ever more likely to be punished.

But he said there were about 20,000 families where the parents had 'lost control of their children' and would be required to sign contracts promising to improve their behaviour. Anyone who didn't would be hit with 'tough sanctions', including eviction, as part of the early intervention initiative which was pushed strongly by the previous premier, Tony Blair.

Knife crime was now firmly on the political agenda, so much so that there was a Commons row about it. Shadow Justice Secretary Nick Herbert said the government were still 'cobbling' the plan together the day before it was published. The document followed six other 'action plans', he said, and added: 'People don't want more last-minute government action plans, they want action.'

He added, 'In the last week three more young people

have lost their lives in knife attacks. After a decade in office, all you can offer is yet another apology and yet another crime plan of recycled announcements and lazy gimmicks.'

Mr Straw hit back: 'You seem to be implying that should there ever be a Conservative government, there won't be any knife crime, there will be no violent murders. I think this is a rash and immature pledge to make. I am deeply sorry about any crimes of violence, as I am about any crime. What we are seeking to do by strengthening the way the whole criminal justice system works, and not least by strengthening support we give to the police and those dealing with crime against youngsters and by youngsters, is to ensure there are many fewer examples of this kind of crime and many more of those who perpetrate it are brought to justice.'

Liberal Democrat President Simon Hughes said: 'Everybody agrees that, tragically, knife crime is now at the top of concerns for all families with teenagers and young adults the length and breadth of the country.' He asked what the courts were doing now to pass sentences which would reduce re-offending and deter others from using knives.

Mr Straw said the next Lord Chief Justice, Sir Igor Judge, had said 'there will for knife crime, even where the knife is not actually used, be tough and appropriate sentences.'

*

As the politicians continued to pledge action, the turmoil continued. A reply to a written question in the House of Commons revealed that in the ten years since the Labour Party had come to power, there had been a 700 per cent rise in the number of blades discovered in schools, from 902 in 1996 to 6,334 in 2006. Justice Ministry figures also showed how youngsters were avoiding jail for sneaking knives into schools. Fewer than one in five offenders in 2006 – just 17 per cent – was given a custodial sentence and though 691 were fined, many would just have been given suspended sentences or community punishments – but figures for this were not provided.

The statistics were in a Commons written answer to Liberal Democrat MP Jeremy Browne, who said: 'There had been promises of tough sentences for people with knives but that does not seem to be happening at all.' However, a Justice Ministry spokesman said: 'Those prosecuted for carrying knives are now almost three times as likely to go to prison as in 1997, and for a third longer. Also, the age for buying a knife has risen from sixteen to eighteen.'

Among the plethora of figures, the National Health Service released statistics showing the number of people hospitalised during violent attacks had soared by almost 30 per cent in four years: figures suggesting the true scale of knife crime could be much worse than had been feared.

Words on the deteriorating knife situation were flying around in Westminster, but they were also being spoken in Bolton.

Superintendent Dave Flitcroft, from Bolton Division of Greater Manchester Police, summed it up when he said: 'Over the past three days we have seen three isolated incidents where a knife has been used, and today we have seen the devastating effects knives can have with the death of a man earlier this morning. I would like to reassure our local communities that knife crime in Bolton remains a rare event, while it always has the potential for tragic consequences such as we have seen earlier today.'

Paul Gilligan's family paid tribute to him even as the politicians were arguing. They said: 'Paul was a beautiful person both inside and out. He was a devoted and fantastic father to Jemaine, Rio and his special daughter – Macie-Moo – and a caring family man. He was a loyal, loving partner and soulmate to Louise and will be very sadly missed.'

His friends describe him as the life and soul of the party, both very popular and well known in the area. Mr Gilligan had daughter Macie-Moo with partner Louise, and sons Jemaine and Rio with a previous partner.

His brothers Craig and Darren Gilligan left a message saying: 'To our kid, I'll miss you pal, you were my best mate, love you loads.'

His close friends, including the Nedderman family, said in tribute: 'This world will never be the same without you, you will never be forgotten.'

Mr Gilligan, known as Gilly to his friends, was well known in gyms in Bolton.

Carl Fisher, aged thirty-seven, who ran the Combat Base in Bridgeman Place, had known him for nine years. He said: 'Everyone at the club is gutted. We just can't fathom it. He was such a top guy – a loving family man. He will be so missed. He was a good mate and a good laugh. He enjoyed boxing but even though he was a big lad, I never saw him throw his weight around.'

Mr Fisher, who also worked as a doorman in the town centre, said he believed society as a whole was becoming more violent. 'As a doorman, I see so much mindless violence. I can't understand what's going on in society. I think it's getting absolutely out of control.'

Another doorman at a Bolton nightclub had summed it all up: nationwide crises, a society on the brink, a haphazard use of sharp metal, a mentality that cares nothing for the lives of others. They were all crystallised in the case of Paul Gilligan.

It seemed that nothing could make his death seem more obscene, but there was a revelation to be made in the middle of January at Manchester Crown Court when nineteen-year-old Leon Craig Ramsden appeared there accused of murdering the father of three. Ramsden, who denied the charge, had been arrested soon after Mr Gilligan was stabbed in his shoulder and chest that summer night.

The events of that sordid Saturday night/Sunday morning were relived during the trial to provide yet another sickening cameo of life in Britain today.

Prosecutor Guy Gozem, QC, told the jury that several witnesses had seen the attack but did not realise Ramsden, of Turnstone Road, Bolton, was stabbing Mr Gilligan as the knife was concealed in his fist.

He said: 'The stabbing was as unexpected as it was brutal. He brought the bottom of his clenched fist – in which he was holding a knife – down twice into Gilligan's body. It was done so quickly that nobody saw the knife – onlookers thought that what they had seen had been strange "back-handed" punches.'

The court heard the two men were seen 'play fighting' minutes before the fatal attack. Mr Gilligan held Ramsden in a head-lock and rubbed the top of his head. Ramsden then left the bar, only to return seconds later and stab Mr Gilligan before running off. Mr Gilligan died soon afterwards from his injuries.

Taxi driver Mukhtar Nakhuda picked up a man matching Ramsden's description outside the Blue Boar pub in Deansgate, Bolton, at about one o'clock on the Sunday morning.

Ramsden asked the driver to take him to the Vogue nightclub in nearby Bradshawgate, and Mr Nakhuda said to him in a light-hearted manner: 'It's only round the corner, why don't you walk?' Ramsden replied: 'I can't be bothered. I've just had a bit of a domestic.'

Mr Nakhuda said he had dropped Ramsden off at Vogue nightclub, but the bouncers would not let him in because they said they could see blood on him. Ramsden got back into the taxi and asked Mr Nakhuda if he could see any blood on him, and Mr Nakhuda said 'No'. Ramsden later went to Courtneys nightclub where the manager, Mark McKendy, recognised him as a regular customer.

Mr McKendy said Ramsden walked straight up to him and shook his hand, which he thought was unusual. Ramsden was then spotted by doorman Shaun Ricketts, who noticed that he appeared to be hiding something in his waistband. When asked what he was hiding, Ramsden produced a jet-black knife sheath. Mr Ricketts immediately stopped Ramsden and asked him if he had a knife. He also pressed his panic button to summon Mr McKendy. Ramsden told him that he was holding the sheath for a friend, and refused to say where the knife was.

Ricketts alerted the police and Ramsden was arrested at around 1 a.m. on suspicion of possession of a controlled drug and then arrested on suspicion of attempted murder when detectives realised he matched the description of the man responsible for the stabbing.

Then came the bombshell that earlier that night Ramsden had written this twisted entry on Facebook:

'I'm twisted at home. My head's up my a***. I feel like killin some 1 need to stay of the hard stuff ha f*** it it's Saturday ha.'

The entry was deleted, but was recovered in the course of the police investigation from a laptop used by a witness to access the site after hearing about the stabbing.

Ramsden's version of events was, of course, different.

He had been on a three-day alcohol and cocaine bender and did not sleep on the two nights before the stabbing. He told defence barrister Stuart Denney, QC, he was upset because he had rowed with his girlfriend and had been drinking heavily.

The jury of eight women and four men were shown photographs on his mobile phone of his two friends posing with knives, and a photograph of him clutching a beer can while snorting cocaine.

Ramsden, who admitted he came from a family of 'troublemakers', said of his infamous Facebook threat: 'It means I'm not feeling normal, I'm not feeling level-headed. It was just a figure of speech, I didn't literally mean going out and doing something like that.'

He said that on 12 July he and two friends snorted cocaine and shared twenty-four bottles of beer and a bottle of vodka before going out to the Pepper Alley bar at about midnight. There, Gilligan, whom he knew socially, got him in a headlock 'which made my nose bleed', and rubbed his head with his knuckles.

He said this made him feel embarrassed and he left the bar shortly afterwards with his friends.

Ramsden said they stood outside badmouthing Gilligan until his friend Reece Armstrong, twenty-four, came out of the bar and passed him a knife and a sheath and told him he had 'stabbed Gilly'.

He said he tucked the sheath into his waistband and handed the knife to an unnamed person and told them 'to get rid of it'.

Ramsden then went to a club on his own, where the sheath was spotted and he was arrested on suspicion of drug possession after two sleeping pills were found on him. He said he did not name Mr Armstrong until the first day of his trial because 'I didn't want to get my mate in trouble.' When he was arrested on suspicion of attempted murder he told police 'you're trying to fit me up because of my dad.'

Window-fitter Ramsden admitted trying to destroy one of his two mobile phones because of the pictures on it of Reece Armstrong with a knife and the Facebook entry he had made using the phone. But his lies were to no avail – he was found guilty.

Sentencing him to life with a minimum of seventeen years in prison for the murder, Mr Justice Teare said: 'Paul Gilligan was thirty-one years old. He lived with his partner and three children. His death has caused great suffering to them and also to his parents and his two brothers.' The judge added: 'This was a senseless and unprovoked murder which has devastated Paul Gilligan's family,' continuing, 'You left Pepper Alley after the headlock and decided to return. You could simply have left the area of the club but you chose to return and stab Paul Gilligan. Nothing Paul Gilligan did could justify or excuse your actions. I therefore do not regard provocation as a mitigating factor.'

Outside the court, Detective Inspector Mark Roters from Greater Manchester Police read a statement on behalf of Mr Gilligan's partner and family.

The family said: 'We'd like to thank the police and all the people involved in the case, who worked so hard for justice to get a young, dangerous man off the streets for a long time. We also want to thank the brave witnesses, jury and all who have supported and prayed for both us and for justice to be done. Ramsden has never shown remorse throughout and thought he was "untouchable". He knew he had killed a man, one loved by many, in a heartless, shocking, cowardly stabbing. Paul didn't deserve nor would have anticipated such brutality. He is greatly missed and was such a happy, social, family man. We will never get over his death and live on to explain the murder to his baby and two stepchildren.'

And in an epitaph that could apply to so many victims of knife crime, they added: 'Knife and serious crimes such as this should carry lengthy sentences.

There should be more random stop-and-searches and education from a young age about the implications these crimes have to deter people from carrying such weapons.'

14

Karl Bishop liked to carry knives. He also had a habit of smirking.

Jobless Bishop was grinning as he sauntered into the courtroom at the Old Bailey in his shabby grey track-suit to hear sentence passed on him. He stood with his hands in his pockets as he was sentenced to life behind bars and smiled at his friends in court even as the words condemning his hate-filled philosophy were coming from the judge's lips.

He'd been smiling eight months earlier on an early-summer's night in Kent. That was the Saturday evening he'd ended the life of Rob Knox, the eighteen-year-old actor from the Harry Potter films. Bishop seemed to think that was all so very funny too.

He was a deadly time-bomb just waiting to explode and anyone who had the misfortune to be near him when he did would suffer. Like so many others who were the victims of knife crime, rugby-playing six-footer Rob Knox was in the wrong place at the wrong time.

Bishop's father had left the family when he was small and the boy was expelled from primary school as a troublemaker because of problems caused by his uncontrollable anger.

It was almost inevitable that the young Bishop would soon be in more difficulties and indeed he was known to the police when he was just fourteen. A year after that he faced charges of threatening a youth he knew with a knife, only for the allegations to be dropped when he appeared in court. It was only postponing the inevitable. Later that year outside a minicab office he slashed the same youth, and that boy's friend, across the face, leaving one needing five stitches and the other with a cut on his nose. So, in May 2005, he pleaded guilty to wounding with intent to cause grievous bodily harm, and causing actual bodily harm and was jailed until March 2007.

After his release he worked fitting air conditioning for a few months before being made redundant, and later worked occasionally as a window cleaner. Bishop's mother worked at a cab firm near to the bar where the lives of Rob Knox and Bishop were to cross with tragic results.

As its address indicates, the Metro Bar in Station Road, Sidcup, is virtually alongside the mainline railway station in that sprawling hinterland where the relentless march of between-the-wars suburban expansion merged London and Kent into one. One customer described it as 'a pretty cool place where you should dress to impress, packed with a diverse and happening crowd. Metro Bar has excellent cocktails that really get you in the mood.' Another put it in less PR-handout terms, saying in a review: 'Awful place full of awful people. Totally brings the area down, chavs on mopeds hanging around outside, people looking to cause trouble and full of orange underage idiots swigging blue WKD. Avoid unless you're 15 years old in which case you might like it!'

Whether it was 'cool' or a meeting-place for chavs – the name given to a seemingly ever-expanding inarticulate underclass – made no difference that Saturday night, 24 May 2008.

A week earlier at the club, habitual cannabis-user Bishop, twenty-one, had for no reason accused Rob's group of friends of stealing his mobile phone. Bishop was punched in the face and went home before he returned, armed with a plank of wood, and announced, 'You don't know who you're messing with. I have put plenty of people down. I'm going to come back next week and someone's going to die.'

That's exactly what happened. It was to be a night of mayhem and a night remembered in the confused, sometimes contradictory, recollections of the young people there.

One of them, Karen Jones, eighteen, was harassed by

the drunken Bishop as the trouble began to ferment and even gave him a peck on the cheek to try to get rid of him, but he said, 'I want more,' and tried to pull her away with him.

'He was asking me for a kiss and I told him "no" and he still wouldn't leave me alone,' she remembers.

'I said no, because I had a boyfriend. He said, "Well he's not here tonight so what he doesn't know won't hurt him," and started trying to drag me away from where I was with my friend. He pulled me by the arm to go away from the Metro Bar but I was holding on to my friend Alice's hands so that he wouldn't have been able to take me anywhere. I gave him a peck on the cheek so he would leave me alone but he said "I want more than that". He was quite drunk. He couldn't stand up straight, he was stumbling.'

She said she managed to get rid of him by saying she would come over and talk to him later, but shortly afterwards she saw him fighting with Rob. Although that broke up she was later told by a friend, 'he's coming back with knives', and she saw Bishop casually stabbing two of Rob's other friends, Charlie Grimley and Dean Saunders.

'He just looked like a normal person walking down the street making out that nothing had happened and then he did that.' She and her girlfriends hugged each other in fear and burst into tears with the shock of what they had witnessed.

Later she was outside Queen Mary's Hospital in Sidcup with Charlie and other friends when they spotted Bishop, who had also been in the mêlée, being wheeled out in a chair. Charlie told Bishop he hoped he would 'rot in jail'. But then, she said, 'He was sitting in the ambulance laughing like he wasn't bothered. He was like, "I don't care, I've been in there before and when I get out I'm going to rape your mum."'

Nicky Jones remembered that night too. At least twenty-year-old Nicky was 'lucky' in that he too was attacked by Bishop, but unlike Rob lived to tell the tale. He had, in his own words, a 'scary' encounter outside a nearby Tesco Express shortly before the mayhem began. Bishop had brandished a knife while angrily shouting: 'What are you laughing at?' But he then went off telling the group: 'It's your lucky night, you're not getting done.'

Nicky made his way towards the Metro Bar where he saw Bishop with his back to the doors, holding a knife in his right hand. He picked up two empty bottles of Smirnoff Ice to defend himself and walked over to him. 'I said to him "if you calm down, I'll calm down," and placed the bottles on the floor. It was as I stood up that he then lunged towards the group and towards Rob. Bishop was shouting, "Who's going to make my fucking day?" and the main target of his threats appeared to be Rob. He was pointing the knife towards him, arms outstretched.'

Another youth punched Bishop, but as he came away Bishop had taken the second knife out. 'It happens really quickly from then. I grabbed Bishop's left hand to try and stop him from swinging the hand round with the knife. I used my right hand to grab his left hand. As I proceeded to grab his left hand, he swung his arm over my head and his hand towards my chest. I raised my left hand in defence to cover myself. The knife in his right hand went right through my wrist and came out between my thumb and index finger. As I'd been stabbed I put my hand up, turned away and as I turned away Rob moved past me towards him.' Nicky was left with tendon damage and had two operations because of the attack.

Charlie Grimley, seventeen, who was also one of Bishop's victims, saw brave Rob Knox dash out of the bar after hearing that his younger brother Jamie had seen Bishop with a knife.

'He was walking at a fast pace – I think it was because he wanted to see Jamie.'

Charlie went outside and saw Bishop holding two knives, while Rob was being held back, shouting: 'He tried to stab my fucking brother.' As the struggle between the two men went ahead he saw that Bishop was swinging his arms. 'Rob was getting weaker. I thought he was hitting him but it turns out he was stabbing him.'

Charlie Grimley had had a foretaste of what was to happen because the previous week he had seen the row between Bishop and his eventual victim. That night the young actor was wearing a T-shirt with the phrase 'Too young to die' and Bishop told him: 'You're not too young to die.'

'He said he was going to be back next week and someone's going to die. He was also saying "You don't know who you're messing with" and "I've put people down."'

No one was safe that night from the scything, flashing blades that shortly before had been nestling inside a suburban kitchen drawer.

Callum Turner, aged nineteen, who visited the bar nearly every weekend, ran to the Metro just before the stabbing to warn people, after earlier being threatened with a knife by Bishop. He, Jamie and Nicky Lee Jones had met Bishop by the Tesco Express: 'He had two knives. He was holding one up at Nick and was also waving one about where Jamie was.' Bishop then approached Callum's car shouting: 'You look like a big man. Come on, big man, get out the car.' Bishop appeared to be treating the encounter as a joke and was waving one of his knives around inside the car.

As Callum Turner quite understandably put it: 'I've never ever felt so scared in my life. I was begging him to leave me alone. I was begging him not to hurt me.' When Bishop headed off towards the Metro Bar he raced ahead of him to try to warn others. 'I'm in hysterics. I'm crying, I'm shouting at the top of my voice.'

But he said the bouncers standing next to Bishop outside the bar just stared at him blankly.

Rob Knox then confronted Bishop with the words that were to be among the last he ever spoke. 'How can you hold up knives to my brother?' Bishop then pulled the knives out and was shouting: 'Come on then, who wants it?'

Callum Turner recalled: 'His face looked like he was thinking "What have I done?" and then it changed again and he was obviously thinking "Right, I've got the knives out." To me it looked like he was just going to stab everybody.'

It was mayhem. Another friend, Andrew Dormer, punched Bishop in the face and as he did so, Bishop stabbed him in the chest. Then Callum Turner picked up a chair and threw it at Bishop only to see it bounce off his shoulder. Rob Knox desperately smashed a bottle over Bishop's head to stop him stabbing another one of their friends, Dean Saunders.

Although Rob got Bishop in a bear-hug and tried to get him into the flowerbed, the killer then stabbed him with both knives what looked like 'hundreds' of times, Callum said, and then several people jumped on Bishop. Callum comforted Rob, who was now lying on the floor outside the Somerfield supermarket, until the police and ambulance arrived. As Callum held Rob he said to him, 'You're a doughnut, aren't you, getting involved in all this rubbish. It's not worth it is it, Rob?'

Dean Saunders remembered little of the attack on him after leaving the bar by a fire exit, but he had been stabbed in the neck by Bishop, suffering spinal damage, and only became fully aware of his condition in a hospital Magnetic Resonance Imaging machine.

Another victim of Bishop's frenzy was Andrew Dormer, sixteen, who tried to disarm Bishop when he arrived outside the bar holding knives. 'He was holding them in front of him, blades pointing up. There was a smirk on his face. I saw him with the knives up and then when he lowered them I saw my chance to get him on the floor, to get rid of the knives.' Then he was hit with a bottle and was also stabbed, although he didn't realise it until he became drowsy.

Others told similar stories of the night: of the hatred and threats, the bravado and challenges, the refusal to back down and the ultimate, inevitable consequence of the damage that knives can cause in the hands of those who don't hesitate to use them or care about the immediate harm they inflict or the immeasurable sadness they leave behind.

No one summed that nightmare scenario up better than Karl Bishop and no one who was there that evil night has better reason to remember it than Jamie Knox.

The tragic irony of that night was that it had started so well; Jamie knew that Rob had been in an upbeat mood as it was just a few days since he had finished filming his role as Marcus Belby in *Harry Potter and the*

Half-Blood Prince and was looking forward to being in the following instalment of the blockbuster film series. The brothers had been so keen to be out and about that evening they had even left home without having time to say goodnight to their mother Sally with whom they lived.

In Jamie's own words Rob was 'very upbeat, very cheerful, always in a happy mood', but sadly for Rob he was also the type who looked after his baby brother. As Jamie put it: 'He looked after me a helluva lot, very protective.'

That was why brave Rob confronted Bishop that night. 'He was shouting. He was going mad, saying "You held a knife to my brother, why did you hold a knife to my brother?" and he had friends holding him back as well and I think there was a bouncer there,' Jamie said. Another youth tried to punch Bishop but he fought back.

Jamie added: 'He was lunging, sort of swinging his arms, flailing everywhere. I believe other people got involved almost instantly. I couldn't believe what I was seeing.' Jamie then saw his brother trying to rugby-tackle Bishop.

'He was slumped into him . . . he had his arms around his waist and his head pressed against his chest to one side.' Jamie tried to help his brother by putting his left arm around Bishop's neck and throwing several punches but he was thrown off in the mêlée and landed in the flowerbed. The next thing he knew was Rob being led off by another friend saying, 'I've been stabbed.' One of those wounds severed an artery in his chest.

Then Jamie had to telephone his mother to tell her what had happened. She rushed to the scene from their home nearby, but the crowd, police and paramedics kept her from reaching Rob and so she had to follow him to the hospital where a policeman gave her the devastating news – her son was dead.

There was no such sorrow or regret from Karl Bishop. He'd gone armed with two knives in the first place because the twisted logic that passed for his thought process said that 'two knives is scarier than one'. At his subsequent trial it was said that he regarded stabbing as 'an occupational hazard' and he carried knives in his pockets the way other men carry pens.

After running amok leaving a crowd of dead and injured young men in his wake he begged police to save him from an angry crowd, then winked and smiled as he was led away. He boasted to police that he had done 'bird' before. 'Take me to f***ing Belmarsh,' he shouted. 'I'm going down anyway, just take me there now. I don't mind. I get gym every day, meals – just take me there.'

When told later that night that Rob Knox had died he replied, 'Yeah, sweet.' His only regret at that time was that boxer Ricky Hatton was fighting Juan Lazcano of Mexico that evening, and he raged, 'Oh, f***'s sake, f***ing hell! I'm gonna miss the f***ing Hatton fight. F***ing hell.'

There was the same lack of contrition at his Old Bailey trial early in 2009. Far from being the aggressor that night, Bishop maintained he was merely defending himself that evening. He hadn't even wanted to go there that night after the previous week's incident, but his friends persuaded him. In his own words of the street he was 'merry drunk but not proper lagging'.

When the trouble began he had no other option but to flail around with his knives, he claimed. 'I was just trying to get away,' was his lame excuse. He said he was scared surrounded by the crowd – 'They were screaming, they were chucking bottles at me, they were just going mad.' Surrounded by the circling crowd with Rob being 'more aggressive', as he put it, than the others, he took the knives out of his pocket.

'As soon as he ran at me everyone just ran at me. I couldn't be exact but there was a few – six or seven, maybe more. I didn't attack them. From what I can remember I was always going backwards and just swinging and trying to keep people away from me, but they just kept coming towards me. You wouldn't think people would run at someone who's got a knife. I didn't intend to wound anyone at all, but they attacked me. There was no other option. They ran at me, they attacked me. They had me surrounded at one point so I couldn't go anywhere even if I wanted to.'

Why didn't he drop the knives? His excuse was, 'They would have been used on me,' adding, 'My aim was to scare people away from me and then as they kept running at me the knife was catching them while they kept running into it. I was just trying to get away ... I'd just been beaten up again – twice in two weeks. My assumption was that it was the same people, as it was the same place, so I was quite angry. I put them [the knives he had gone home to collect] in my front pockets. I just wanted to scare whoever was down there. I wasn't really thinking that straight at the time because I was so angry, pissed off.

'I was regretting what I was doing, that it could have all gone wrong – and it did,' he said, claiming he was about to go home when he was surrounded and the final bloody chapter of the night began.

He admitted a red mist had descended on him during that night and said, 'I didn't care at the time. I wasn't thinking at the time. I wouldn't have expected people to attack someone with knives. It's idiotic. I didn't intend to use the knives. If you show knives to people they are normally quite scared. I would be. I wasn't the one being aggressive. They were the ones being aggressive. I was surrounded. There were bottles coming from all angles, so I took the knives out so they wouldn't come near me. I might have said "If anyone comes near me I'll stab you", but that's because I didn't want anyone to come near me. They [the knives] were there so I took them out. At that point I wasn't intending to use them but I ended up using them. If I went to the ground I could have been the one dead.'

He continued to claim that he didn't want to hurt anyone but that begged the obvious question: why had he stabbed poor Rob Knox no fewer than five times? In a grim understatement he did eventually admit that that was 'over the top'.

Prosecutor Brian Altman, QC, pointed out to the Old Bailey jury at Bishop's trial that the accused stabbed at least six men eleven times during the course of the mêlée, in the full knowledge he would cause them serious harm.

'This man was the aggressor and he was acting out of revenge. He knew that there was no need to resort to violence. He had brought the whole thing upon himself quite deliberately.'

'He had the whip-hand. He was the one armed with and using two knives.'

The prosecutor compared the injuries Bishop had received – cuts, grazes and bruises – with the wounds he had inflicted on others and how the crowd had acted to disarm Bishop and 'stop him stabbing others'.

He said: 'What else were they to do – stand by and watch this man swinging his knives around as clearly he was?'

Mr Altman added: 'This man carries knives like others carry pens in their pockets, quite happily thinks little or nothing of stabbing others as if it were some occupational hazard.'

And in words that capture not just the horror of this case but the brutality of the growing knife epidemic, he added: 'Carrying knives is abnormal, it is not permitted, it cannot be done. It is not glamorous, it is not normal and it is not lawful. People get seriously injured and people die – as this case all too tragically demonstrates.' He said Bishop, a 'habitual knife-carrier', was trying to suggest 'people were throwing themselves at him like lemmings. Courageous or foolish perhaps, it doesn't matter because they were trying to do what they instinctively thought was best in a highly dangerous and volatile situation.'

He told the jury that the defence was asking them 'to endorse the carrying of knives', pointing out the statement by witness Scott Shorter who said Bishop shouted before the mêlée: 'I told you someone was going to get hurt. I'm going to stab someone.'

Mr Altman's conclusion was: 'This was a loss of temper by a very angry man who we say was bent on revenge, bent on showing those youths at the Metro Bar exactly who they were messing with.'

Justice was done when the jury found Bishop guilty of murdering poor Rob. But there was no way that anyone could make Bishop feel ashamed of his acts. The day after the verdict he swaggered, hands in scruffy grey tracksuit pockets, into the dock for sentencing. He had refused to be there when the impact statements from Rob's family were read, but his 'courage' had returned by the time sentence was passed on him and he grinned at three of his pals in the gallery and even giggled on one occasion.

He was sentenced to life and told that he would spend at least twenty years behind bars for Rob's murder; he was also given three concurrent life sentence for wounding Dean Saunders, Nicky Jones and Charlie Grimley with intent to cause grievous bodily harm, and two years for wounding Andrew Grimley.

Judge Mr Justice Bean called him a 'very significant' danger to the public, telling him: 'You are a highly dangerous man. I do not think it is proved that you intended to kill Robert Knox. The truth is that you simply could not care less whether you killed him or not. When you learned you had killed Rob, your only response was to say, "Yeah, sweet". Your lack of regret, let alone remorse, was truly chilling.'

If the heartache of the Knox family was not great enough, when the verdicts were announced it also emerged publicly that two months before the Metro fight, complaints were made to police that Bishop had attempted to rob and then burgled another youth.

The victim's mother had named Bishop to police but he was not charged after the youth said he did not want to give evidence against Bishop, who was, of course, known to use knives. Given his past record, if he had been arrested there was a probability that he would have been in custody over the incident and not free to cause the havoc that night at the Metro. But he wasn't tracked down or questioned. Two police officers were subsequently given written warnings after the Metropolitan Police carried out an investigation and found standards had not been met.

A police statement said: 'The Met. realised the existence of this earlier allegation to police concerning Karl Bishop would concern the family and the public. The Met. acted promptly to address this by asking its Directorate of Professional Standards to investigate, also voluntarily referred the matter to the IPCC, which supervised the investigation. A thorough investigation was carried out and as a result two officers involved in the robbery investigation were given written warnings. Lessons have been learned from what happened in this case and measures have been taken, including the introduction of a new system to help monitor and arrest outstanding suspects for all violent crime offences, including knife crime. The Knox family was kept informed of this DPS investigation throughout and of all measures taken as a result of its findings.'

As always, it was the family left behind who had to cope and then come to terms with the agony that a knife attack brings.

Rob's mother Sally, fifty-one, was typical of those who suffered in such a way, if 'typical' isn't too mundane a word for such an event.

After the case, both in her impact statement and in conversation, she expressed her feelings in the most honest, heartbreaking manner:

As a mother and parent I can never forgive the person responsible for taking my son Robert's life, or the devastation that has been caused by these actions. Being a mother I am fully aware of the effects of our loss of Robert, not only on myself and Colin as parents, but more so on Jamie, Robert's younger brother. Jamie has not only lost his brother, he has lost his best friend, confidant and protector. I really wish that no other family have to suffer and endure the loss of a loved one at the hands of someone with a knife.

We will work towards making sure he did not die in vain by continuing our work against knife crime.

You can never comprehend the loss or hurt caused by the death of a child – a child that was wanted, carried for nine months and encouraged and supported through childhood to a young man. As a parent you hope and believe you will not outlive your children. And although you appreciate that in some instances this is not possible due to illness, it is crueller when their life is taken away by the actions of another person.

I miss him so much . . . if only I could turn back the clock, give him one more hug, take one more look at his face, tell him how much I love him.

She recalled the beginning of that night and how Rob, Jamie and their pals were so excited about going out.

They were so excited they went out without saying goodbye. How I wish Robert had popped his head around the door to say goodbye. I really wish I could remember the last moment I spent with him, that last look. But this was cruelly taken away from me when he died.

Sally felt 'panic and fear' after Jamie called her to say Rob had been stabbed. And she rushed to the scene: 'I wanted to go to him, speak to him, comfort him, hold him. But I wasn't allowed.'

Sally followed on when Rob was taken to hospital, and her husband Colin, from whom she was divorced, joined her in a waiting room. 'I will never forget the worst moment in my life when a police officer and a doctor walked in and told us Robert had died. I wanted to die myself – I couldn't believe it. They were talking about my boy, who hours earlier had been chatting and laughing in the kitchen.

'All I could think about was just wanting to see Robert, kiss him, tell him he would be OK. I cannot explain what it is like living without Robert, the hurt of not being able to have a chat with him, not being able to cook and look after him.

'I miss him so much. I wish we could laugh together again, I could moan at him for being untidy, lying in bed – the normal things in life. You can never comprehend the loss or hurt caused by the death of a child. It is crueller when their life is taken away by the actions of another person.

'I wish we were in America where life means life. I don't think in twenty or thirty years, when he is released here, he will be any different. I just hope he goes to a prison that will make his life a misery.

'I hope he suffers, but nothing can make me feel any better about not having Rob here. Bishop has made no apology – I don't think he is capable of it. But even if he did I wouldn't believe it. If he was sorry he would have pleaded guilty. Instead he tried to injure us more by putting us through a trial.'

And she was justifiably contemptuous of Bishop and his refusal to be in court when the family's statements were read.

'I just saw the guy for what he was, a coward. He had been so cocky and arrogant, but finally lost face when he refused to hear the impact statements. I wish he had been forced to come in and hear those words, after all he has put us through.

'I was surprised that never happened, but I don't think it would have made any impact on him anyway. He has no emotions, no heart. He is dead inside.'

Rob's father Colin suffered a parent's anguish too. He

said the last time he saw his son was in the hospital chapel: 'He looked asleep. So I told myself that he was only sleeping and that the angels will take him to heaven. If anyone earned a place in Heaven, it was Rob.

'We are enormously relieved justice has been done, although there is nothing that will compensate for the shattering sense of loss.

'His life was stolen, taken without permission. He was taken in the most cruel way possible. His life, love and kindness will never be felt again . . . I won't get to see him become engaged and go on to get married. Nor will his brother now be able to be best man at his wedding. I miss him so much it breaks my heart. All I have are memories to remember him by.

'It was on that day my son was taken from this earth. His life was stolen, taken without permission, in the most cruel way possible. His life, love and kindness will never be felt again by his mother, brother, father, nans, grandad, aunts, uncles, cousins and friends. Robert had many attributes. Loving, caring, thoughtful, generous and kind. He had just been fortunate and successful in his acting.

'When he got the part of Marcus Belby in *Harry Potter and the Half-Blood Prince* he was so excited, happy and proud. The intensity of his absence is sometimes unbearable. Living my life without my son in it is like having a daily nightmare. Those that have nightmares will wake up in the morning and say,

"Thank God it was only a nightmare" and their life returns to normal.

'I live my nightmare daily. I wake up to the fact that my son is not here for me to hug, kiss, laugh with, talk to, text or phone.'

Heartbroken Colin added that not a day went by when he did not cry for his son. He said: 'It could be at work, on a train, watching TV or in bed. There are nights I lie in bed for hours not being able to sleep. I talk to Rob every day. I know he is beside me right now. He has been with me ever since his death. I talk about some of the things that we have done and could have done.'

He recalled: 'When he was born and he came home to his first house, I took him in my arms and walked him into the garden. He was wrapped in a little blanket and I said, "Robert, welcome into our life. I will love you and I promise to take care of you and protect you." I have done so for eighteen years.

'I never had the chance to say goodbye to my son. I had to go to the chapel of rest at Farnborough Hospital. I had to stand over him and talk to him without any life in his body. I didn't want to leave him, but as I said my farewell, I bent to kiss him. He was very cold.' But I told myself he was only sleeping and that the angels will take him to heaven. If anyone earned a place in Heaven, it was Rob.'

Colin, too, had his own damningly frank condemnation for Bishop's refusal to stand in court and hear the family's feelings towards him, his crime and their loss.

'I thought, "You spineless, gutless, coward. Now everyone knows what you are." That was one of the worst things. There was no sorrow, no regret and no respect for our family. I hate him. I hate what he has taken from me and I hate how he acted in that court room. He's nothing more than a scumbag and I don't like to waste time thinking about him.'

Colin told how the family had to move Rob to another school at the age of thirteen after appalling bullying because he was overweight. He said: 'Hearing that your child is sad or upset, or that people are hurting him is heartbreaking.

'As a parent you are meant to be there to protect your children, but you can't just walk into a school and do what you want. So we took him out. From then on Robert was a confident person and loved his acting. When he was cast for *Harry Potter*, it was one of his proudest moments. Me and his mum tried to keep him a bit grounded. We didn't want it going to his head too much. He was really enjoying life. Him and his friends would go out to bars, dress up in waistcoats and the like and drink champagne.

'He loved it and really had a good time and I'm glad he did, because he didn't know what was just around the corner.'

Younger brother Jamie too was, of course, devastated by the loss of his big brother. He said: 'Rob was my brother but he was also my very best mate. Nothing can ever replace him and I hate that guy for what he's taken from me.'

Jamie, also an actor with appearances in TV programmes including *The Bill* and *A Touch Of Frost*, said: 'We had the same group of friends, did the same after-school activities like tae kwon do and shared a love for acting. Every memory I have has Rob in it. For my whole life he was there and that's what I find so difficult – that someone has taken him away so quickly.'

He remembered his brother's joy at landing the *Harry Potter* role: 'He'd been getting a bit down because I'd got a few jobs recently and he hadn't. When that one came about he was over the moon. There was a little bit of jealousy because I would have fancied a job like that. But mostly I was just so pleased for him. He was just thrilled to bits.'

Jamie added: 'Rob died protecting me like he always did and I am so proud of him. That's the sort of person he was and who I remember. He would always want to make sure I was OK. I couldn't face looking at Bishop until the moment he was sentenced. Then I couldn't stop staring at him. No sentence will ever bring Rob back, but the only thing that would come close to being satisfactory would be if life meant life. I want Bishop to die in prison, not be free to pick up his life where he left off in twenty years. Rob's gone for ever, so should his killer.'

A private funeral service for Rob had been held at Eltham Crematorium a month after he died and later that day there had been a memorial service at St John the Evangelist Church in Sidcup. Friends from Rob's D and B School of Performing Arts sang his favourite pop hits, 'Wonderwall' by Oasis and 'Shine' by Take That to the packed church whose mourners included Harry Potter star Rupert Grint (Ron Weasley in the film series).

In the wave of justifiable public horror that surrounded both Rob's death and Knox's trial it would be naïve to ignore the connection with the *Harry Potter* movie. It was this link that propelled the stabbing into the newspaper headlines and onto television screens.

So it was fitting that one of the last tributes paid to a young man who had died long before his time should come from the *Harry Potter* cast and crew who had been devastated by his death. They wrote tributes inside a copy of the J.K. Rowling book upon which the film was based. Rupert Grint wrote a note too, saying: 'Rob, it was an honour to have known you and whenever I'm on the Southend strip I'll be thinking of you. Rest in peace mate.'

And the star of the film, Daniel Radcliffe, wrote to the family too, saying, 'Dear Rob, We are all proud to have known you and devastated to have lost you. It is terrible just to write this note. Rest in peace, Dan xxx.'

Below it he had written a message originally from *Lady Chatterley's Lover* author D.H. Lawrence, who had sent it to a friend in 1923. 'To everyone else who reads this remember: "The dead don't die. They look on and help."'

POSTSCRIPT

The word 'knife' already existed in a recognisable form in the English language even when William the Conqueror invaded these shores in 1066. Like the word, the object itself has stood the test of time. The ability to make and use sophisticated tools is one of the reasons why mankind has prospered over all other species on the planet, and what better tool than a knife? So easy to transport and so useful for building, clearing, cutting, defence and many other valuable, creative purposes. Handy for killing too.

Knives have been used to commit acts of violence for thousands of years. In the Old Testament's Book of Judges there is a detailed description of how, in about 1200 BC, the Moabite king Eglon was stabbed to death by the left-handed Ehud with a long, concealed blade. Over a millennium later Julius Caesar died in an orgy of more than twenty cuts and thrusts on the steps of the Senate in Rome in what is still the most infamous knife attack of them all. A barbaric mob-slaying in a crowded public place for all to see in its bloodstained, gory detail. Sounds familiar? Swap the Senate for a busy shopping centre or a forbidding, graffiti-covered housing estate at dusk and it could be a story told from the grubby pages of everyday life in modern Britain.

So why should it be any more worrying or different today than it has been in the past? What has changed in the lives we lead in the current world that somehow a danger that once seemed remote is apparently drawing continually closer?

To suffer from a stab wound, either slightly or fatally, was once a prospect that appeared to most people like an aeroplane crash or an earthquake. Of course things like that happened, but always to another person. Nowadays no one can be quite so certain, so confident and secure that whatever terrible events are about to occur will 'happen to someone else'. Everyone now knows that the victim on the evening news or pictured in the morning papers in happier times could easily have been them.

And what can be done to stop this disease reaching epidemic proportions? Amid accusations of 'massaging' of statistics to hide the true enormity of the problem, some may argue that the battle is being won, but try telling that to the innocent soul being eyed by a group of feral, hooded youths on a darkened street, or a teenager racing desperately through the night to escape from a gang attacking him for some unknown, motiveless reason. Try telling it too to the growing number of parents who have lost a child, someone they loved beyond description, who left home one day as usual never to return. Their feelings of dread can't be assuaged by homilies or campaigns, politicians' sound-bites or platitudes.

The growing use of knives and their nonchalant acceptance by more and more people, especially youngsters, cannot be separated from the rest of the problems faced in an overcrowded, urban country where values are changing so rapidly in so short a space of time – far from it.

Knife crime, of course, cannot be viewed in isolation, it is yet another symptom of a larger illness in society. The perpetrators of the crimes examined in this book have common themes running through their lives: poor literacy levels, absent fathers, broken homes, no possibility of fruitful, rewarding employment ahead – even if it were wanted, which it usually wasn't – gang membership seen as the only way under-achievers can attain any status or respect from their peers. Drug misuse and alcohol-induced aggression too are all there time and time again, a predictable formula whose components may alter from time to time but whose eventual outcome is depressingly similar.

None of these factors, nor any other deprivations, should or could excuse the terrible crimes committed, even though they may form part or all of the reasons for them. If that were the case then there would be literally hundreds of thousands of knife-wielding thugs continually rampaging through the streets in a never-ending wave of terror. It isn't quite that bad, not yet anyway.

But it is from this ever-growing section of society that virtually all the perpetrators of knife crime come. The use of a steel blade to instil terror and carnage is not a white-collar crime; the educated, affluent, aspirational middle classes don't 'do' knives. It's a good job they don't, given the number of young men and, indeed, young boys of frighteningly few summers, who do and who seem to have no reluctance to use them aggressively for the slightest twisted reason. A lost generation indeed!

All this leads to one terrifyingly obvious conclusion: that the greater the ills in society, the more our education system fails to prepare young people adequately for life and the lack of plentiful, rewarding work opportunities, then the greater the problem of knife crime will become, invariably growing proportionally alongside other social malaise, or possibly increasing at an even faster rate.

Of course there are those who call for tougher restrictions and harsher sentencing, and these could well be among the ways of combating the menace. Any measure that reduces those mind-numbing statistics of knife attacks and murders or possibly saves the life of just one potential victim is worthwhile. But will such steps alone be enough?

There are some deadly weapons, guns being the most obvious, that, thankfully, are not easy to obtain unless money is available or the potential user has access to a network or individual who can provide them. But that cannot be said of a knife. Knives are available in every kitchen drawer in the land: lethal implements nestling alongside the egg-whisks and bottle-openers. They can't be locked away, only for use on special occasions. Knives are all around us and to change that situation would be like uninventing the wheel.

What can be addressed, however, is the propensity of some people to use them for evil. Only through better education in all areas of life, not just the school classroom, can an increasingly violent mindset among so many be halted and, hopefully, reduced.

As one of the senior police officers involved in combating the menace so succinctly put it: 'In any crime-reduction approach the first thing to do is arrest the increase and turn that cycle around. This is a long journey. Success when you're dealing with these sorts of problems might be measured in generations, not weeks or months.'

Let us hope, for all our sakes, that the answer is found before it is too late.